ESKIMO ADVENTURE

ANOTHER JOURNEY

NTO THE PRIMITIVE

by

Edward L. Keithahn

BONANZA BOOKS • NEW YORK

Copyright © MCMLXIII by Superior Publishing Co.
Library Of Congress Catalog Card Number: 63-152-14
All rights reserved.
This edition is published by Bonanza Books
a division of Crown Publishers, Inc.
by arrangement with Superior Publishing Co.
a b c d e f g h
Manufactured in the United States Of America

Dedicated to

TONI

TABLE OF CONTENTS

TABLE OF CONTENTS—Continued

LIST OF ILLUSTRATIONS

LIST OF ILLUSTRATIONS—Continued

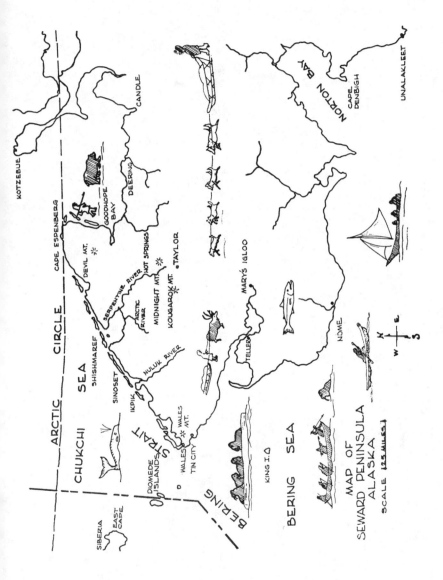

MAP OF
SEWARD PENINSULA
ALASKA
SCALE (25 MILES)

Chapter I

ON OUR WAY

When Toni and I shoved off for Alaska back in 1923 we were not stampeding to a new *Eldorado* or *Bonanza Creek*. We were simply embarking on a two years' teaching job that was going to pay me $1200 per year, and Toni $800. This wasn't very much money even in 1923. In fact we had resigned jobs back in the States that paid much better. But there was this difference: where we came from a man and his wife were not permitted to teach in the same school. Moreover, very few married women could even get jobs. So if we were going to get married and get any use out of our brand new life diplomas we had to look for new diggings.

There were four alternatives. We could go to the Panama Canal Zone, the Philippine Islands, Hawaii or Alaska. Now Toni had been reared in the hot Yakima Valley from which her family had fled to the cooler clime of Puget Sound. She didn't relish the idea of going to the tropics where Yakima's sweltering summers would be an aggravated daily fare. That left Alaska. So we applied for a job to William Lopp, Chief of the Alaska Division of the Bureau of Education and were accepted for a station in the Arctic with the unbelievable name of *Shishmaref*.

I had a few vague notions about Alaska, for my grandmother went there when I was a small boy. She lived in Valdez, stampeded to Iditarod and drove dogteams. She sent us many postcard views of these towns and other places, mostly featuring dogteams and deep snow. I heard her speak of Nome—which I immediately confused with Rome—and I remember her mentioning Judge Wickersham frequently as if he were some sort of demigod. That, plus a hazy melange of Eskimos, polar bears, auroras and the midnight sun, was about the sum total of our collective knowledge of Alaska in the spring of 1923.

Toni and I were in San Diego at the far end of our honeymoon when we received a telegram from the U.S. Bureau of Education Offices in Seattle stating that our ship was sailing in just five days. *Five days!* And here we were 1500 miles from Seattle in a wobbly 1920 Model T Ford coupe. How we made it in time I'll never know. We hardly left that car on the return trip. When night came and we were too tired to drive farther, we would just pull off the side of the road and sleep. Then at the first sign of dawn we would take off again. On reaching Seattle we sold the car to the first taker for $50 which was just about our entire capital.

Luckily, we had credit and were able to purchase a two years' outfit that very day. Since neither of us had ever done any housekeeping, we hadn't the slightest idea of what we would need or how much we would use in two years. We were directed to the Schwabacher Bros. Wholesale Grocery Company. There they assigned a salesman to us who was supposed to know all the answers, he being a family man and all that. He did a pretty good job, too, but we never did find use for the ten pounds of dry mustard he sold us for making mayonnaise. The tub of sour pickles would also have been pretty much of a dead loss had the Eskimo kids not taken a liking to them. Besides the groceries, we picked up trade goods to barter for meat and fur clothing, some guns and ammunition, bedding and so forth. At last we were all set.

The first view we had of our ship was something of a shock. We had been told where it would be lying but, when we got to the dock, it was nowhere to be seen. There were ships in the Alaska trade all around; the *Queen* lay at her berth and we saw the *Admiral Rogers*, the *S.S. Yukon* and some others, but no *M.S. Boxer*. We were on the verge of panic, believing it had gone off without us, when we happened to glance over the guard rail. Beneath us we saw a small craft bearing the name *Boxer*. Relieved, we guessed the *Boxer* must be somewhere about for here was her tender. We were still waiting for the *Boxer* to return from the oil dock or elsewhere when other prospective passengers began to congregate in little groups nearby. Crewmen with their ditty bags arrived and slowly the truth began to jell. This dinky hull was no mere tender. This *was* the *Boxer*!

Typical landlubbers, we had assumed that the farther you travel, the bigger the boat. We were bound for a village in the Arctic, 3000 miles away. Naturally we had expected something in the *Queen Mary* class. We had long since forgotten—if we ever knew—that the *Mayflower* was only ninety feet long.

The *Boxer*, formerly a barkentine-rigged naval training ship, had an overall length of 120 feet. Recently it had been turned over to the Bureau of Education as an Alaskan supply ship, after which it was converted into a diesel auxiliary schooner. This was to be its maiden voyage with, Captain S. T. L. Whitlam, veteran

Arctic pilot, in command. There must have been a minus tide when we first saw the *Boxer*, for some hours later our ship had risen ten or fifteen feet and looked far more seaworthy. The tiny, so-called staterooms were all beneath the deck which was entirely covered with sacks of coal, drums of gasoline, and stacks of lumber. The only clear place for standing was the hatch cover, or the top of the pilothouse. This was to be our floating home for the next thirty-three days.

Late that night we cast off. Most of the passengers had long since retired to their narrow berths, tired from the last hectic day in port. But Toni and I lingered on deck until Seattle's twinkling skyline faded in the distance. We were on our way.

Morning found us in an unfamiliar region of smooth waters, gray skies and timbered islets. The scene varied little during the next four days. It was like going up a broad river, hemmed on both sides by timbered slopes that got steeper and higher each day. Always there seemed to be a choice of routes, as large islands or headlands appeared and fiords opened up to the east. Perhaps we did take the wrong channel occasionally, for Captain Whitlam was a deep-sea pilot unfamiliar with the inside passage and he had a green crew. We even included Bella Bella among our ports. On the many trips up the Inside Passage since, we never again saw Bella Bella. It was not on the regular route. How we got there on the *Boxer* I doubt we shall ever know.

On the fourth day out of Seattle we pulled into Ketchikan— by virtue of its location, Alaska's first city. It didn't remotely resemble the Alaska we had in mind. Except for a slightly wilder aspect, it could have been a port in the state of Washington. Perched precariously on the rocky slopes of Deer Mountain, with its foundation in the mud of Tongass Narrows, Ketchikan was a typical Southeastern Alaska salmon-canning town. It had an odor pretty much its own, one that in later years we were to grow very fond of. Better known as *gurry* smell, this odor came from the decomposed offal of canneries, where thousands of salmon were butchered and their refuse dumped into the bay, to be stirred up by the propellers of every ship that docked. A sailor told us that *Ketchikan* in translation means "stinking place where ships lean to seaward." Of course this was nonsense but however humorous to a tourist, would insult any loyal Alaskan. It would insult me now but on that day I thought it was funny. I was a *cheechako*.

We had docked at Ketchikan to replenish our diesel fuel which from that point had to take the *Boxer* to Barrow and back. There was barely time to rush up town, snap a picture of Chief Johnson's totem pole, then scurry back. The *Boxer* threaded its way northward to Sumner Strait and through that broad passage westward to the open ocean. Morning found us out of sight of land, heading across the heaving waters of the Gulf of Alaska.

Before many hours had passed, it was not the sea alone that heaved. All of us did, including the captain and the crew. That is, all but an Eskimo girl and an elderly Scotsman, neither of whom missed a meal on the whole trip. We others, in our collective misery, all agreed that the Scotsman was no better seaman than the rest but was just too tight to give. As for the Eskimo girl, she remains a mystery, for in later years I learned that most Eskimos get desperately seasick the minute they board a rolling ship although the motion of a kayak or oomiak in the roughest seas bothers them not a bit.

As we advanced across the Gulf, the weather grew worse and our top-heavy craft began doing frightening things. Piece by piece, the deckload went overboard. The lumber was the first to go. Drums of gasoline and assorted cargo followed quickly. The seasick crew didn't even appear on deck. Tex, who signed on as an able seaman but was actually making his first voyage left the wheel for the rail at an inopportune moment. The *Boxer* slid into a deep trough nearly dipping her masts. Scuttlebut spread that the *Boxer* had once capsized off Havana. When a 100-gallon oil drum broke loose and came crashing below deck into the dining salon, luckily there was no one present but a caged parrot. The oil drum ripped up the table and made kindling of the chairs before it was captured and made fast. Meanwhile, the parrot cage had been rolling hither and yon, in bilgewater and out, with the feathered occupant shouting sailor invective we never before dreamed was in its vocabulary. Many hours passed before it resumed language fit to be heard by schoolteachers and missionaries.

Without captain or crew well enough to work the ship, it was hove to and for the next three or four days wallowed, willy nilly. Then the storm abated, the seamen recovered, and we got under way again. Finally we came into the lee of the Trinity Islands west of Kodiak. Calm seas brought the wan, haggard passengers on deck. Whales and porpoises now appeared in great numbers and the air was filled with goonies, gulls and sea parrots. We landed at King Cove for water, coasted easily down the peninsula until we entered Unimak Pass then headed northwest again into the Bering Sea.

Rounding Unimak Island was a treat, the first real thrill of the voyage. Here was an island that might have been picked out of Northern Japan. It was barren of everything but grass, yet out of its rolling, grassy plain rose numerous symmetrical, volcanic cones. The two tallest were *Pogromni* and *Shishaldin*, perfect Fuji-like cones with eternal fires smoking at their tips by day and casting a dull, red glow by night. The shallow waters of Bering sea wiped out the long swells of the gulf. A slight chop bothered no one, and the dining salon again was popular.

With wind and weather perfect for sailing, the sails were unfurled and the diesel was shut down. How wonderful it was to sail noiselessly and seemingly without effort. At times the silence was deafening and we would keep swallowing in an effort to restore hearing only apparently lost. Often only an albatross was visible on the ocean breast. Then again we would come upon vast masses of whalebirds sitting on the smooth, glassy waters. Occasionally we spotted a whale rising to blow and momentarily disturb the surface. When we neared the Pribiloffs, however, the sea became a mass of black, bobbing heads. These were fur seals that rendezvous here each summer while their young are born and reared on the nearby islands.

St. Michael was our first port of call on the Bering Sea and here we debarked the Scotsman and his little wife. They had been so quiet and unobtrusive the whole voyage that we had hardly become acquainted with them. The couple was well past middle age and the quiet little lady and her knitted shawl reminded us of Whistler's mother. We wondered how they would keep warm the coming winter.

St. Michael showed merely a shadow of its early importance as a Russian outpost and later as a port for Klondikers who chose the river route to the rigors of Chilkoot Pass. The old Russian fort still bristled with primitive iron *pushkas* whose authority must have derived more from threat than from action. A Russian Orthodox church was in semi-ruin but still proud and dignified in its Byzantine bulb. There were also a few pitiful Eskimo huts of sod and salvaged lumber, and the abandoned barracks of the American military post, with its large ware-

houses near collapse. Saddest of all was the clutter of beached
river steamers dating from the Klondike stampede, now out of
business because of the newly-opened Alaska Railroad. We went
aboard the *Hannah,* the *Susan* and the *Sarah,* twin stackers,
each already falling apart but still resplendent with gay hand-
painted murals of the nineties.

All that remained to keep St. Michael alive was the post of
the Northern Commercial Company. Serving as distribution
point for the lower Yukon Valley, it still enjoyed a healthy business judging from its bulging warehouses and diversified stock.
Aside from Mr. Williams, the N.C. Company manager, the only
person of importance we met in St. Michael was *Reindeer Mary*
who was also known as Sinrock Mary. She had acquired a sizable
herd of reindeer and was reputed to be the wealthiest Eskimo in
these parts. I can still see her friendly smile, the twinkle in her
intelligent eyes, and the three vertical blue stripes tattooed on
her chin.

Our next stop was at Unalakleet on Norton Sound, the first
genuine Eskimo village we saw. At last we felt we were really
entering the Alaska we had dreamed about. Here we were greeted
by dozens of red-cheeked, smiling Eskimos, and seemingly hundreds of yapping malemutes all straining at their chains as if they
longed to tear us apart. The natives reassured us as they came
forward with outstretched hands, each of which we pumped cere-
moniously as was the custom.

Charley Traeger was the local white trader and postmaster
and more or less general contact between these people and the
outer world. His log-constructed establishment was also the
social center of the village. Nearby was the deserted *kazhgie,* a
former Eskimo social center. The store, mission, and school had
taken over its function. We saw several frame dwellings with
kitchen gardens, but the majority of the habitations were of
driftwood and turf construction, semi-subterranean to with-
stand the winter blast. Russian influence seemed negligible,
though several of the families had Russian names.

When we arrived in the roadstead before Nome a day later,
all early ideas of similarity between that famous northern metrop-
olis and Rome vanished instantly. Here were but the bones of
what had been a golden mecca for thousands of fortune seekers
only twenty-three years earlier. It was as if a gigantic vine had
sprung up near the mouth of Snake River and had grown lustily

up and down the beach, nurtured by the golden sands. Now the gold was gone and the vine, dying at the ends, had withered and retreated to its original roots where feeble life still existed. The town was miles long and seemingly only yards wide. Great stretches of large, unpainted warehouses were empty. Only a few blocks were inhabited by something less than a thousand people. We went up town and registered at the Golden Gate hotel for the sole purpose of having a bath, our first since leaving Seattle.

Nome was a friendly place, for all its meagre population. It was here that we first met Bishop Peter Trimble Rowe, whose diocese was the largest in the world, and Clarence L. Andrews, the Alaska historian. We also met Judge G. J. Lomen, whose sons, Carl and Ralph, were making Reindeer history. Then there were Frank Martin, a fur buyer, Tony Polet, who traded in carved walrus ivory, and Charley Jones, the U.S. Marshal whose deputy I was to become in a curious incident two years later. That same day we saw Captain Roald Amundsen getting ready to take off on a flight over the North Pole, with, as he boasted, "only a six-shooter and a sandwich." Later we learned that he decided to abandon the scheme. He went instead to Italy to build the *Norge,* with which he and Umberto Nobile made the successful flight over the Pole in 1926.

New friends drove us out to the third beach line where huge dredges scraped the bedrock eighty feet below the surface for gold too deep for the equipment or capital of ordinary miners. We went aboard the *B. Desperate Hyde,* a huge *Yuba* dredge floating in its self-made lake. There we watched the bucket line bring gravel up to be washed in a huge cylinder for gold it contained. Here was gold mining without glamor. The few men necessary for its operation explained the shrunken city.

At Nome, Mrs. Corinne Call, pioneer Alaska schoolteacher, debarked with her brood of adopted Eskimo daughters. Coming aboard were Superintendent Charles Dupertius of the Nome office of the Bureau of Education and C. L. Andrews bound for a teaching post at Kivalina.

The village of Wales at the entrance to Bering Strait was our next stop. This pitiful hamlet crouched at the foot of Wales Mountain as if to fend off wintry blasts that roared down the barren slopes. The tiny buildings were half of lumber and tar paper, a new idea, and half of driftwood and turf. Most of these dwellings were empty and falling in decay. Only a few years earlier Wales had been a prosperous village of 800 but the flu epidemic, which reached its northern limit at this village, had reduced the population to about 250. Of these, some fifty orphaned children had been removed to Teller Mission on Port Clarence. The village was dominated by the schoolhouse, a large alpine-type frame building that included the teachers' quarters and Post Office as well.

We had hardly landed when a large crowd, principally middle-aged women, centered on Chief Lopp and did not break up until we departed. Lopp had been stationed here as a missionary in the nineties and his children had been born here. He could converse with the Eskimos in their own tongue and there was much to talk about. No doubt many of the women clustered about him had been his students twenty-five years before.

Another group was centered about a lone Eskimo somewhere in his thirties, who held a tiny, two-year-old child in his arms. The singular thing about the little girl was her fiery red hair. A poker-faced sailor off the *Boxer* was kidding the Eskimo.

"Peter," he asked, "whose girl is that?"

"That's my girl," said Peter with finality.

"No, Peter, that can't be your girl. It's got red hair."

"That's my girl," returned Peter doggedly, holding the child closer.

"Well, Peter," said the sailor, "can you prove it's your girl?"

"Sure, I prove it all right," said Peter.

"Well, prove it then," said the sailor.

"All right," said Peter. "I'm a trapper. I set trap. Pretty soon fox in that trap. Whose fox is that?"

"Why," said the sailor, "that's your fox."

"All right," said Peter. "This my girl!"

While the freight was going ashore by skinboat, we walked through the village and up the western slope of Wales Mountain. Wild flowers grew profusely here, among them pixie-eyed primroses and arctic poppies. It was a clear day and the Diomede Islands were visible in the middle of Bering Strait. Beyond them only fifty-six miles from where we stood was the gray Siberian coast, as forbidding and sinister as the stories of atrocity and horror already coming across the channel by the mukluk telegraph of the Eskimos. Little did we suspect that we ourselves would later play a part in one of these bloody stories.

That evening, in the broad daylight of the arctic summer, we headed northward through Bering Strait and into the Chukchi Sea, that segment of the Arctic Ocean which held our future island home. That night we tried to get some sleep knowing that the morrow would bring much work getting our goods and school supplies ashore and becoming established in our new home.

Our plans went awry when we found that the cargo had been improperly loaded and our freight, including all our personal effects, was buried under tons of other freight for points farther north. It was impossible to get at ours. The captain gave us a choice. Either we could complete the voyage to Barrow and debark southbound, or we could take a supply of ship's stores now and get our own supplies in a couple weeks. We chose the latter plan since we had an overwhelming desire to be landlubbers again after thirty-three days on the crowded *Boxer*. Consequently we were dumped into a large oomiak, along with a two-weeks' supply of groceries, then hurried ashore without breakfast or so much as a single cup of coffee. Captain Whitlam was not one to cater to lowly schoolteachers.

Chapter II

OUR STATION

The village of Shishmaref had looked forbidding from the deck of the *Boxer*. It was situated on Sarichef Island, a detached sandbar some three miles long and less than half a mile wide. Both ends of the island were barren even of grass, but the center, rising some fifteen feet above sea level, consisting of a series of sand dunes, captured and held by rank-growing wild rye grass. On top of these dunes were lesser knobs and humps that were the sod igloos or *eenies* of the Eskimos. In the middle of the cluster rose two frame buildings. One of these was obviously the school-house. It was faded box-car red and equipped with an uncovered bell. A whitish square building about the same size, some sixty feet to the right and bearing a flagpole, proved to be the teachers' cottage. At least one thing was certain. Small, run-down, and mean as it was, we would have the best house in town.

The village was deserted when we arrived since it was the custom of these people to spend the brief summer in the hunting camps scattered along the beach from the mouth of the Nuluk to Cape Espenberg. A few hunters, though, had sighted our ship approaching the village and had followed it in to earn a few dollars lightering the freight ashore and longshoring. For about five cents a box they carried our meager effects to the cottage and helped us get settled. They assured us the people would soon return to re-occupy their *eenies* and then we could start school. Wild and shaggy as they looked in their skin clothing, we were assured by their kindly smiles and twinkling eyes. These were good people; there could be no doubt about that.

The teachers' cottage consisted of only four small rooms but was adequate. It was roughly furnished with the basic necessities for housekeeping in the Arctic—all on a scale slightly better than that of the leading natives. The walls, floors, and ceiling were insulated with shredded paper and the windows were double-glazed except on the north side where they were triple. There were a living room, bedroom, kitchen, and storeroom, the latter also housing a chemical toilet, though an outdoor privy was provided for summer use. For lighting we had a hollow-tube gasoline pressure tank system that operated gas mantle lamps, but not very well. Water was not provided. In summer you carried brackish water from a pond; in winter you sawed ice from the same pond and melted it for use. The fuel for the kitchen range and the potbellied stove in the living room was Utah coal, but our coal had been carried on with the rest of our outfit. A quick look in the coalshed revealed we had precious little left. If the ship didn't return on time, we chanced resorting to sealoil lamps like the natives.

It was now the middle of September and the Eskimos were returning. Instead of moving into their igloos at once, they set up tents nearby. Then the men began getting the huts in shape for occupancy. They cut new sods to replace sections that had eroded since last fall and replaced torn gut windows. They brought vast quatities of native foods and hides from the beach, where they had been dumped from the oomiaks. These they stored in the caches standing behind or beside each igloo.

One by one, the villagers—by some pretext or another—began dropping in to get acquainted with us. Usually it was for *martizan.* We soon found that as dispensers of free government medicine and medical supplies we were much more in demand than as educators. The new medical supplies were aboard the *Boxer,* but there were still ample supplies on hand of vaseline, epsom salts, cathartic compound, tonics, and elixirs. Most of the requests were for these simple remedies. Besides the cabinet of medicines, the station had a fairly good assortment of medical books, including one especially compiled by Dr. Daniel S. Neuman for use by isolated teachers who must serve also as doctors and nurses. It soon became apparent that whatever medical attention our village was to receive would have to come from us. Considering the state of our collective medical knowledge at the time of our arrival, this was not comforting. So, to help make up the inadequacy, we read over and over again all the bookshelf contained on the care and treatment of everything from rickets to gunshot wounds.

Our nearest doctor was at Nome, some three hundred miles by trail. We might as well have been living on the moon as far as outside help was concerned. We fitted out our small leather Boston bag—popular in those days as an overnight bag—with an assortment of medicines and supplies, in anticipation of house calls. Looking back, I am sure the psychological effect of that bag and its mysterious contents did more to heal our sick than did the treatments we gave. At any rate, tension around the sick bed seemed to relax when we entered the room and began our diagnosis. In those first months we felt we didn't dare fail. Later we found that the Eskimos were sensible people who did not regard us as miracle workers and would look upon the outcome of our endeavors as fate or God's will. Always we would take the temperature and the pulse of the patient and observe whatever other symptoms there were. Sometimes, if the father was present, we would ask questions and get helpful answers, but most of the women spoke no English.

Generally we could diagnose and prescribe a treatment on the first visit. Some cases, though, required more reading of the medical books. In every case we administered the treatment personally so we always knew if and when the patient received the medicine. We were probably just very lucky but in two years we didn't lose a case. The patients would probably have recovered anyway yet we had the satisfaction of knowing we didn't do them any harm.

Our first case was pitiful. We were barely settled when a family arrived from its summer camp and established itself in a tent on the lagoon about half a mile from town. One day two little girls came in to tell us that their baby sister was awfully sick, "maybe dead already." Following their lead, we accompanied the girls across the soggy tundra to the small camp. Inside the tent, on a piece of folded reindeer skin, lay a motionless child about two years old. Her mother squatted beside her crying softly. We could see that life had already left the tiny body. The eyes and lips were sealed and the body was cold. One little fist was closed tightly on something. I gently opened the hand. Within it were several small sticky pieces of hard candy with straws clinging to them. This was the last loving offering of these people, known throughout the world for their love of children. We were never to know what might have become of this child had it been within our power to save her life. But her older brother was later to become Alaska's foremost Eskimo artist, George Aden Ahgupuk.

Two weeks passed, then three; still no *Boxer* returned. Our food supplies were rapidly dwindling but we borrowed a shotgun and shells and eked out our supplies with an occasional duck or ptarmigan. In the attic we came across some ancient packages of dried vegetables and Gold Nugget desiccated, granulated potatoes. Probably dating from the Nome gold rush, these vegetables defied all attempts at soaking, remaining rubbery even after cooking. They served admirably though, for seasoning our roasts, stews and soups which we concocted from local wildlife that fell victim to our shotgun.

Meanwhile we had employed several women to manufacture our arctic wardrobes: fur parkas, mukluks and pants; dogskin mittens, sealskin water boots and reindeer sleeping bags. For the parkas we had purchased prime August reindeer skins in Nome, where Lomen Brothers provided a large selection. August skins are better for parkas than those taken earlier or later in the year because the hair in August is neither too short nor too long and is not likely to shed. Hides from young deer show, in places, a little wool-like curl which marks them as choice. Sleeping bags are made of later skins when the hair has grown longer. The result in a warmer sleeping bag. This warmth can mean life or death when one is caught on the trail in a blizzard as we later learned.

Since all Eskimos have short, broad feet, my size 12AA amused the woman who made my mukluks. She measured for length, apparently using the same proportions that she did in making boots for her husband. The finished mukluks were about fourteen inches long and nearly six inches wide. Even after being properly lined with straw, they could still receive my feet wrapped in half a gunny sack, with room to spare.

Water boots are the mukluks you wear in summer when the tundra is just one big, soggy marsh. They are of hairseal skin, dressed without hair, and have soles of oogruk leather. The oogruk is a large, bearded seal with extra-thick hide. If well made, these water boots are paper light and absolutely water-proof. For this reason, both whites and Eskimos prefer them to rubber boots. In fact, much of the money income of this village derived from the commercial manufacture and sale of water boots. So well made were the Shishmaref boots that they commanded a premium of fifty cents over those of other villages. We paid three dollars a pair for knee-length boots and four dollars and a half for hip boots, using barter goods instead of cash.

Speaking of cash, we found out—as Eskimos had long before our time—that money hasn't much value in the Arctic. What is needed there is merchandise: food, clothing, medicine, ammunition, kerosene, soap. One old villager known as Koppe-zuruk told us about his first experience with silver dollars. It was around 1900 and white men, attracted by the gold discoveries on the beach at Nome, had gone farther north seeking new bonanzas. They were gophering on every creek and beach in the country. One day Koppezuruk met such a prospector on the ice. The white man, using sign language, made Koppezuruk understand that he wanted the seal on the Eskimo's sled. Eskimo-fashion, Koppezuruk gave it to him as a present. The white man thereupon gave the Eskimo a handful of "big, silver buttons with eagles on them."

"But," said Koppezuruk, laughing gaily, "they had no holes in them so I threw them away."

Ningneoluk, another old man of our village, was different. He was a successful trapper with the reputation of a miser. He would accept gold or silver coins for his furs, but no currency. Once I asked him why, since the other trappers would take it and traders accepted checks or paper money as readily as coin. Ningneoluk looked at me steadily with narrowing eyes and said softly, "Fire will burn it. Mice will eat it."

One crafty fur buyer discovered that most Eskimo trappers would accept, not only currency, but a reasonable facsimile thereof. This man had several thousand checks printed in denominations of five, ten, and twenty dollars in green ink, closely resembling currency. Since his business reputation was good and solvency unquestioned, anybody, including whites, would take the checks as readily as they would Uncle Sam's notes and treasury certificates. From experience this fur dealer knew that those checks would circulate in the Arctic until they wore out and few would ever come near the Seattle bank on which they were drawn. Meanwhile he would have ample time to sell the furs and bank the proceeds. Besides having his business largely financed by the trappers, he could enjoy the hope, and perhaps the realization, that now and then fire would burn and mice would eat his checks.

Although we had very little money and no chance to draw any from our salaries under the conditions, we didn't seem to need it. Occasionally we had a chance with some passing traveler, to send an order to Nome. Lomen Brothers could always be relied upon to pick up for you what they could not supply from their own huge stocks. Sooner or later—by Eskimo trapper or deerman or an occasional white—the package would show up, but not with a bill. Never could we get anyone in business in Nome to send us a statement of what we owed. If we would protest, the answer was always the same, "When you go *outside,* that will be soon enough," and what's more, they meant it.

Outside had a new meaning for us in Alaska. It wasn't simply the opposite of *inside;* it was the opposite of *Alaska.* Any place but Alaska and the Yukon was *outside.* Everybody settled up their accounts when they left the country but there was no particular hurry to collect small accounts so long as they were good. And they remained good as long as you stayed in Alaska.

In the state of Washington we had used the term "over the hump" or "east of the mountains" to indicate the eastern part of the state which lay beyond the Cascades. In Alaska the region beyond the coast ranges was the *Interior.* And people who lived in Southeastern Alaska or "The Panhandle" referred to all points west of them as "to the Westward." However, when they referred to the "West Coast" they meant only the west coast of Prince of Wales Island. Of course, we learned all this some years later because the inhabitants of Arctic Alaska didn't know the *Panhandle* existed. As a matter of fact, the white residents north of Nome hardly knew of the existence of Seattle since they habitually wintered in the San Francisco Bay area, principally in Oakland.

*   *   *   *

Another week slipped by. Still no *Boxer.* The days were getting very short and steadily colder. Already little pans of slush ice were forming in the salt water; hordes of hair seals, oogruks, and walruses were going south. The birds also were leaving us. Every day enormous flights of snow geese, emperor geese, whistling swans and little brown cranes passed overhead, their multiple wedges aimed at Bering Strait and points south. Most numerous were the eider ducks of four species that at times almost filled the sky. Then there were brown-throated and yellow-billed loons that flew like guided missiles. Out came the kittiwakes and other gulls, parasitic jaegers—sinister birds—old squaw ducks with their whistling tails, scaups, scoters, and pintails. All were leaving us. Little shorebirds like jacksnipes, phalaropes, sandpipers, plovers and golden curlews rested briefly on our islet, then flitted on in pursuit of the stronger fliers. It was enough to make one wonder why we people lingered when every wild thing that could swim, fly or run was getting out of the country and getting out fast.

Chapter III

OUR SCHOOL

By this time, tents had been taken down and cached, igloos had been repaired and re-occupied and thin, blue smoke could be seen rising from those that could afford a fire. We decided to open school on the first of October, supplies or not, and to keep it going as long as the coal held out. On the opening day, I rang the school bell loud and long, with no idea yet how the local populace felt about white man's education. In fact, we, ourselves, had seriously begun to wonder what we could offer these people of any value to them.

Before nine o'clock our one-room school was filled far beyond its normal capacity with sixty-eight mukluk-ed and parka-ed youngsters ranging in age from six to perhaps twenty-five. They represented about a quarter of the population of the village and a brighter, healthier-looking group of children would have been hard to find.

Our first concern was finding out where each one belonged on the educational scale. None had a report card or any other evidence that he had been exposed to book learning, and the station records told nothing. Gradually, by one means or another, we found that none had advanced beyond the fourth grade. So, we divided the students into two groups separated by an imaginary line passing through the middle of the room and our oversized pot-bellied stove. Toni took over the beginners and second graders and I took what was left, including several who were older than I was.

All our students were bright with the exception of two or three who were amiable but just plain stupid. The rest were eager to learn and learned rapidly. We could but wonder why, in a village with such intelligent people, almost no one spoke English —yet there had been a school here for sixteen years. Little by little we found the answer. In the first place, many of the teachers had been missionaries in the pay of the Bureau of Education, through a contract arrangement with various missions. They were not trained teachers and, in some cases, they themselves had not gone beyond the fourth grade.

School consisted of the singing of hymns and the memorizing of Biblical memory gems. Apparently considerable time must have been given to penmanship for, almost without exception, the Eskimo children were beautiful penmen. And, sing! Most of them sang like larks. We even had a boy who could play the organ with mittens on. This was a useful accomplishment because we often opened school with the room temperature still ten degrees below zero. On those frigid days the breath of the singing children would fill the room with a heavy fog and soon the frozen desk tops would be snow white. Since penmanship always followed singing, the older children who used ink would hold their bottles in their hands, alternately blowing on them and singing. When I could see that enough ink had thawed I would start the class. Instead of using pen or pencil, the smaller children printed their letters in the frost on their desk tops, a warm finger functioning as the writing tool.

Another explanation as to why English was little known or used lay in the Eskimo teachers of that era. They were usually family men of better-than-average local scholarship who were employed when missionaries or professional schoolteachers were unavailable as was often the case. To them, school was something that operated only when there was nothing more pressing to occupy their time.

Station records consisted of lined cards, perhaps four by six inches in size. On these cards the teachers were to account for the twenty-four hours of each day including Saturdays, Sundays and Holidays. One of these cards left at our station read in places something like this: "No school today. Shortage of wood in village." This would be followed by several sets of ditto marks. School would then resume for a day or two. Next came, "No school today, sickness in teacher's family." After a week of sick-leave, school would be resumed, followed soon by, "No school today. Seal hunting," or, perhaps, "sickness in village" or "shortage of seal meat" or "trip to reindeer herds" or some other very good reason why the school should be closed.

After seven or eight months' school term of this nature came four or five months of vacation during which the families scattered to hunt, gather, preserve, and store the necessities of life. During this time everything learned in school would be unused and forgotten. So the net result was that each year the students, and teachers as well, started from scratch.

We had our disruptions, too, although infrequently. I remember the day, shortly after we had opened school, when we heard a great commotion in the vestibule and in burst a group of men brandishing wicked-looking spears, harpoons, rusty shotguns and rifles. They shouted something to the big boys who, without so much as "by your leave" leaped up and rushed out the door on the heels of their elders. Imagining the Siberians had landed, I rushed out too, grabbing my Luger enroute. I joined the band racing toward the beach, each heavily armed and grim-visaged. Along with the rest, I leaped into a skinboat still wondering what was up, since I could see no enemy. We were rowed swiftly out to sea where we presently found ourselves in a large pool of diluted blood out of which the tall, black dorsal fins of several killer-whales circled. Then someone reached over the side and retrieved the floating carcass of a young *beluga* or white whale which at this age was pearl gray instead of white. The killers had attacked and cut to bits at least one *beluga* which accounted for the sea of blood. But the young one must have been struck a heavy blow which killed it and only our timely arrival prevented it from being swallowed by those voracious wolves of the sea. Eskimos liked to eat them too, I could tell by the happy expressions of the returning party.

As time went on, and we learned a little of the language, these incidents were less shaking but always exciting. Gradually, we became a part of the little world of Shishmaref and what was happening in the other world that we had left, paled into insignificance. We were too busy to be homesick.

Then one day we heard the joyous "*tray-may, oomiak-puk, kah!*" of the natives, which heralded the approach of a ship. Sure enough, laboring toward the village on the distant northern horizon we could see the *Boxer,* long overdue. The sobering thought, however, was that we knew it couldn't land our cargo. A northwesterly wind was blowing a gale and a ten foot surf was breaking on our beach. Moreover, the spray was freezing and had built up a barrier six to eight feet high that would have to be negotiated, somehow, whenever a lighter reached the beach.

Opposite the village, the *Boxer* dropped its hook and waited about a mile off shore. The storm did not abate and night fell. We wondered if it would wait out the night or pass us up. Morning found it still anchored but the storm continued to rage all day and again night fell with nobody daring to attempt to reach it. We could hardly hope the ship would stay with us another night but it did. That morning a group of men called on

Their smiles were universal.

Toni in high shoes and parka "spring outfit."

In my trail outfit.

Our schoolhouse after the paint job.

Our school kids.

Our home.

Our house in the winter's blast.

The *Boxer*.

Returning from the *Bear*.

The schooner *C. S. Holmes* on July 8, 1924.

Revenue cutter *Bear*.

A typical malemute sled dog.

"Red," our Kobuk malemute.

Our shipwreck shelter.

Shishmaref before the snow flew.

Our reindeer corral on Arctic River.

Inflated sealskins painted with blood—being prepared for food storage.

The *Twins* and the new *Silverwave* at Teller.

The sea kicks up occasionally.

My hunting kayak was so small I needed a bootjack to get out of it.

Landing an oomiak through frozen spray.

Orville bails our dory.

Some 5000 reindeer in this herd.

Our herd with antlers in velvet.

Coiled baskets made in school of native grasses.

Racks of drying oogruk meat.

Three native children and Toni with four large swans.

Seal hunters return and are greeted by their wives.

me. They said they would be willing to try to reach the ship if I would go with them. Why they wanted me to go along I'll never know but since I had nothing to lose but my life I said I'd go along if they thought they could make it. Besides, I was the only one in the lot who could swim and that probably gave me a sense of security that I know now was unjustified.

Getting the big oomiak into the water was quite a feat. It took split-second timing to get through the enormous breakers right side up but we made it. From then it was like a ride on a Coney Island roller-coaster without the popcorn. One moment we were riding on the crest of a wave, the next we were at the bottom of a deep trough out of sight of land. It seemed minutes before we would climb out again to a pinnacle from which we could again sight ship and shore.

Eventually, we reached the *Boxer* only to find that in the heaving sea we could not board her. Someone tossed a note to me, attached to a chunk of coal. It was from Mr. Lopp and stated that they would try to put over whatever we needed most. Then the *Boxer* would run to the lee of the Diomedes to wait out the storm, after which they would return to unload our freight. I thereupon made out a list of essentials, tossed it aboard, and they were presently tossed down to us along with a few sacks of coal for ballast. We made it back to the village without mishap and the *Boxer* lifted her hook and sailed away.

*   *   *   *

Now the village became the scene of intense sealing operations. Every man in town owned at least a few fathoms of seal netting. This was a homemade net of seal rawhide with an eight-inch mesh. The operation was cooperative, all the sections being fastened end to end into a net that stretched from shore several hundred fathoms to sea. Twice a day the men would go out in a skinboat to pick the net. Hundreds of hair seals were taken this way. Sometimes an oogruk or a beluga would come afoul of the net and rip or roll up fathoms of it. But the sealers kept a watch for happenings like that and sometimes got out to the net in time to spear or harpoon these large beasts that were capable of escaping or ruining the net if given time. On occasion, if I was free, I would be invited to help pick the net and to shoot with my Luger any large creature that threatened to destroy it.

Periodically the net had to be taken ashore and dried else it

would get too soft even to hold a seal. The hair seals taken in
these nets were cast, whole, into pits where they soon froze. Then,
during the winter, they would be removed one by one as needed,
thawed out and skinned, the meat being used principally for dog
feed. Such meat, known locally as *choked* meat, contained all the
blood of the seal and was not too inviting for human consumption. Besides, fresh seal could be shot at the blow-holes all winter
to provide human food.

Chapter IV

WINTER COMES

Winter was progressing rapidly. The weather grew colder and the winds more violent and continuous while snow and ice covered the frozen tundra. Daylight had shrunk to a couple of hours at midday and the rubbery sea ice was getting thicker each day. Even the ground swells from the north, laboring under the increasing load, were flattening out and slowing down.

Then one morning we awoke in a new world. The marine ice had congealed and the sea was motionless. The almost incessant wind had died out completely and a great silence invaded our land. It was as if we had suddenly been transported fifty miles inland, for it was now that far distant to open sea water. The temperature dropped to thirty degrees below zero but it seemed warmer than it was at minus fifteen degrees when the wind was blowing.

Some things in one's environment are seldom noticed until they are gone. For example, sound and motion. We had come to accept and ignore the lapping of the waves, the murmur or whistle of the winds or even the dancing of a spear of grass. We missed the cries of the gulls when they were stilled, the faint impersonal twitter of the shorebirds and the yap of the malemutes. One sound seems to inspire another and there was nothing now to cause a dug-in sled dog to bestir himself from his nest. Even the people disappeared and were seen outdoors briefly, only when departing or arriving from some distant scene of seasonal activity.

The great change was all for the better except for one thing. We knew now that we had seen the last of the *Boxer*. What would happen to our personal things, our winters' supplies, the school supplies, the coal, and the Eskimos' personal orders that were still aboard? It was anybody's guess.

The change in seasons had brought about a similar change in the Eskimos. Over night they had changed from drab marine hunters, dependent on the kayak and oomiak, to a tribe of terrestrial hunters and trappers free to travel in any direction now with dogteam and sledge. For now summer's mosquito-ridden tundra had become a vast plain of hard-packed snow over which dogteams were free to travel at will. Now the waterboot, the sealskin pants, and sealgut parkies gave way to more picturesque costumes of fur. The fur mukluks were made of alternate vertical strips of brown and white deerskin with snow white or brown straps and topped with bands in geometric designs of deerskin, with bright wool drawstrings and tassels. Fur pants were of brown deerskin, and parkas were of spotted deerskin or of *siksikpuk,* the northern hoary marmot, with hoods trimmed in wolverine and wolf mane. Here, at last, were the storybook Eskimos we had expected to see in the first place.

The first of December found every able-bodied man and even some women taking off for their trapping grounds. The prices for fur were high, even in terms of the traders' goods which were priced something above double the Seattle price. Red foxes were bringing from $22.50 to $25.00 and whites from $30 to $40. Blues and silvers were from $75 to $250 depending on quality but few were brought in. A good cross fox would bring $50 and up. I can no longer recall the prices paid for mink and otter but the mink taken in that area were too coarse to bring top prices.

Our principal fur-bearing animal was the white or *arctic* fox. This animal is gray during summer and towards fall begins to replace its gray coat with a snow white one. It is also a migratory animal up to a certain point. Coming in from the north, the arctic fox doesn't reach the Shishmaref area until it is entirely white, so very few if any of the second-grade *bluebacks* are trapped. Before the season is over it has again passed through the Shishmaref district northbound and is still snow-white. The result was that the Shishmaref catch of arctic fox was about the finest one could find anywhere and always brought top prices. Since a good trapper with any luck at all would catch 30 or 40 foxes, not to mention a few mink, ermine and land otter, it was clear that the trappers were being better paid than the school teacher and making it in three months, at that. It was something to think about, especially with the coal supply running out.

*   *   *   *

The Holiday Season

About the middle of December we began to hear or at least feel faint murmuring to the effect that Christmas was coming. After our Thanksgiving dinner which had consisted of four fried smelt we had about decided to give up our white men's institutions for the time being. But now these Eskimos wanted to celebrate Christmas. We hadn't expected this but we soon found that Christmas week was the biggest event in the whole Eskimo year. So we began preparations for the celebration sofar as the school was concerned. Our students already knew every Christmas song in the book by heart, so the music part was easy. Then they wanted to make a Christmas tree. We wondered about that, too, since where we came from one went out into the forest and cut down a tree and took it home and decorated it. Besides not one of these children had ever seen a tree of any description. To them, a Christmas tree was something you built, made, fabricated; not something you found growing. So we stood aside and let them make it. They started with a ten foot pole, a piece of driftwood someone had thoughtfully saved for the occasion. This was mounted so it stood upright. Then the older boys set to work drilling rings of holes in the pole at about eight inch intervals the whole length of the pole. Someone else who knew Christmas was coming had brought in a sledload of willow branches from the Serpentine River where a low brush grows. These were now carefully driven into the holes in the pole so that they stood out like branches. By setting long branches in the lower holes and shorter ones as they proceeded upward it was not long before the skeleton of a nicely-formed Christmas tree took shape. Then someone reminded us that in our attic there were several discarded green window shades which we soon produced. These were ripped into strips about an inch wide and then cut into six-inch lengths. Then a host of youngsters, armed with scissors, folded these lengths and clipped them into what would pass for spruce needles at ten feet. These were now tied on the naked willow branches with loving care. The process took several days but when the job was completed it was a beautiful Christmas tree, the more so because they had made it from scratch.

We lacked glass and tinsel decorations, candles and colored electric lights. Who had ever heard of electricity, anyway? But the tree was made gay with festoons of local cranberries and popcorn and numerous ornaments contrived from red and green crepe paper. Our young charges gazed upon their Christmas tree as if it was something fresh from Heaven.

On the 18th of December a native from Wales drove in to Shishmaref with a sledge-load of our missing freight. At long last

we had heard of our goods. Everything had been dumped at
Wales back in October when the *Boxer* gave up trying to make a
landing at Shishmaref, and went home. Word came late, since
the channels had only recently frozen, making the trip from
Wales possible.

Now we had a freighting problem on our hands. Besides our
own two or three tons, there were the school supplies which
included 25 tons of coal, and a large shipment of goods which
was to have been the initial stock of the newly-organized native
co-operative store. To freight all of this over an eighty-mile,
unmarked trail by dogteam was quite an undertaking. We held
a few meetings with share-holders of the co-operative to decide
on a course of action.

The Eskimo method of settling a problem is to let anyone
talk on the subject as long as he wants to. There are no comments
or interruptions. And whether you understand the language or
not, you soon are aware that these men are natural born
orators. I had never heard arguments propounded so forcefully
and dramatically. They all enjoyed rapt attention. But when the
last orator had spoken his mind nothing happened. They just got
up and went home.

An Eskimo is not one for hasty decision. He has to sleep on
it first. But, after about three sleeps, they came up with a plan.
Nayokpuk, the storekeeper, and I were to go to Wales and open
the store there. The stockholders, who were also trappers, would
not be adverse to swinging fifty or a hundred miles off their
route and over to Wales to do their shopping. That settled the
problem of freighting the store goods. The rest would be sledged
in by anyone coming our way with an empty sledge for which
they would be paid by the pound in Government barter goods.

Nayokpuk and I took off the morning of the 23rd. He had a
fast team of eleven malemutes so we made it to Sinoset, a distance
of 25 miles, by noon. We had a cup of tea and a biscuit for lunch
and threw the dogs a herring apiece for encouragement. The
trail, which followed the beaches of the string of detached sand
dunes skirting the mainland, was flat and fast, there being only
about six inches of hard-packed snow. After lunch we went on to
Ikpik, fifteen miles farther, where we made camp for the night
in an unoccupied igloo. Here we cooked up a mush of cornmeal,
seal oil, and frozen herring for the dogs and made a hot meal
for ourselves.

I found out a lot about mushing on that trip, my very first of any consequence. For instance, one would not have believed he could dogtrot forty miles in one day without serious after effects. However, I found that exhaustion doesn't stem from muscular activity so much as from getting over-heated. Trotting along at about five miles per hour in thirty degree below zero weather was an ideal combination. I felt about as fit at the end of the day as I had at the beginning of the trip and awoke next morning without an ache or a pain. We still had forty miles to go but we were still a dozen miles from Wales when we agreed to call it a day. Wales sits at the base of Wales mountain which is something of a weather breeder. Anyway, a terrific blizzard was blowing from all directions and we could see no point of bucking it as nothing would be accomplished that evening, anyway. So we holed up in a deserted igloo and there I spent my first Christmas Eve in Alaska.

The evening was not wasted, however, for we were at *Mitliktavik,* the scene of a story that Nayokpuk proceeded to tell as soon as we were settled for the night in our sleeping bags. It seems an Eskimo hunter encountered a polar bear nearby and fired at it, apparently to no effect. Before he could reload the old flintlock, the bear was upon him. Bruin grabbed the rifle, broke it and flung it in the snow. The hunter ran for his life but the bear soon caught up with him, close enough to slap him with the back of his paw, tossing the Eskimo high in the air. Before the hunter descended, the bear was under him again. He had barely time to run a few steps when the bear slapped him in the seat of his leather britches again, sending the luckless hunter up in a high arc before him. This was repeated again and again until the poor Eskimo fell exhausted on his back with the polar bear on top of him.

The big white bear made no further attempt to molest the hunter but just sat on him. The Eskimo wracked his brain trying to think of some way to get the bear off. Finally he thought of something. He took a deep breath then blew his breath right in the bear's face with all his might. At once the bear got up, walked a few steps away and sat down. He may have been puzzled or just plain gagged. Anyway it gave the Eskimo time to get up and run back to where his broken musket lay. He found that he was able to repair it, and when it was again ready and loaded, he came back to the bear. "Mr. Bear," he said, "if I go into the village and tell them what has happened to me they will call me a liar and I will be in disgrace the rest of my life. So I have got to shoot you so there will be proof for my story." Thereupon and with many apologies the hunter killed the bear and returned to his village. He immediately told the people about his encounter and as he had predicted, nobody would believe him. So he took the doubters out to the place. Written in the snow was the scene of the encounter—where he had met the bear, where it had first struck him, where he had landed, where he had been struck, again and again, and where he had lain with the bear on top of him. Then he showed his trail back to the broken gun and his steps that led to the carcass of the bear. The doubters were now convinced of his veracity and the hunter lived in honor and respect the rest of his days.

Morning found the storm still raging so we put on all the clothes we had, put flank protectors on the dogs and took off. Either Nayokpuk drove by instinct or the dogs could smell the trail. At least I could see nothing but swirling snow until we were greeted by yapping dogs at the first igloo in Wales. Nayokpuk was taken in by friends and I found sanctuary with the schoolteachers, a Mr. and Mrs. Nylen. Our stay was as short as possible since we hoped to get back to Shishmaref before the week's Christmas festivities ended. We found a man to operate the store, then loaded our sledge with 600 pounds of most needed supplies. Early next morning we headed for home.

In the twenty-four hours spent at Wales the weather had taken a decided change. It had suddenly warmed into what is known locally as a *December thaw*. It was now snowing furiously and the trail which had been so firm was now a drifting mass of deep,wet snow. It became necessary for Nayokpuk to harness himself into the team ahead of the lead dog to break trail and to help draw the load while I pushed from behind. Fourteen hours later we pulled into Ikpik, all but done in.

The following day was even worse. There was only an hour and a half of semi-daylight this time of year, and because of the storm no stars or moon were there to substitute. Since the trail lay partly on beach and partly on the sea ice, there was always the danger of encountering an overflow or even open water in the channels. Occasionally, Nayokpuk would stop and hack a hole into the trail with a hatchet and study the material in an effort to determine if we were on beach or sea. But the mixture of sand and ice in varying proportions gave only a faint clue. Either we were on the beach or near it, as blowing sand often covered the sea ice as soon as it was solid. We missed Sinoset completely although it couldn't have been by far since our trail followed a narrow strip of sand between the sea and lagoon. Then we saw a black patch in the sky which generally indicates open water beneath. So we veered to the right and kept on.

Fifteen hours passed like a nightmare and now the dogs were whining and occasionally stopping completely and curling up in the trail. Nayokpuk would drag them to their feet with a blast of Eskimo invective and we'd plod on in silence.

Then a curious thing happened. Off to the left, and seemingly in the snow, I saw a light. It was a fuzzy, nebulous glow that seemed so close that I tried to put my foot on it. But it seemed always just out of reach. I called to Nayokpuk who, seeing it for the first time, let out a shout of joy and turned the dogs in its direction. As we went on the light gradually rose higher and the fuzziness left it and it became clear. An hour later we reached its source. We had already passed the village but the light that brought us in was from a Coleman gas lamp hanging in the schoolhouse window, illuminating the Christmas festivities still in progress. As we pulled in to town the light went out, for it was midnight and the festivities were at an end. And thus ended sixteen hours on the trail that had no marker.

December thirty-first was election day at Shishmaref. For a couple of thousand years at least the Eskimos had gotten along without chiefs or formal law. But now, out of deference to some crusading schoolteacher, they had instituted a council whose president officiated as mayor of the village. The men elected, apparently without opposition, were all prominent oldsters who took their offices seriously and officiated with great dignity. Each wore a broad band across his chest lettered "Councilman" except the mayor whose band of office read "President." Council business involved herd laws for dogs, alignment of igloos along a *street*, the construction and care of privies, (a new institution) and the erection of aids to travelers, etc.

The privies are worth description since I doubt anything like them could be found anywhere else in the world. Because the ground is permanently frozen they could dig no holes that would be practicable. So the privies were erected on piling, the bigger the family the longer the poles. After the four poles were set, a small house was built at the top, from ten to twenty feet aloft, as the case might be. These outhouses were walled with burlap from discarded coal sacks and roofed with the same material. Entry to the privy was by tall and shaky ladder. A certain amount of privacy could be had for a time, but Arctic winds soon tore the burlap to shreds or carried it away altogether. Still these unabashed villagers mounted their little thrones to sit each day as nature required and shout greetings to passing friends.

*   *   *   *

AN OUTLAW ESKIMO

Storybook Eskimos are all paragons of virtue and just about the nicest people in the world. In our brief acquaintance with several hundred of them, we had to agree with the storybooks. They were simply grand people. But, alas, there were exceptions. One, we had heard about almost immediately upon arriving. His name was *Avessuk* and according to our informants, he was a real bad man. So bad, in fact, that he never showed his face in the village until the sea was frozen and the Cutter *Bear* had gone south. He wasn't afraid of any Eskimo that ever lived, but he did fear white law men. We heard, vaguely, that he was a murderer, having done in several persons, and would make me much trouble when he returned to the village. He was expected any day now. For a while they had us real worried as I didn't know what I could do with a man who had the whole village bluffed. Then I began to sense that the strong feeling against the man really stemmed from quite a recent event. It seems a whale had drifted ashore and a party of five men had found it and together had cut out the whalebone. Avessuk had elected himself to transport the baleen to Nome, sell it, and share the returns equally with the others. What he did was to take the whalebone to Nome, sell it for $2500 and keep it all. Nobody else got a dime and nobody had the courage to do anything about it.

One Sunday while we were attending the Eskimo version of a ball game at the edge of the village several men with fear visibly written on their faces came up and told me Avessuk had returned. He was already in his igloo. I had long since made up my mind to deal with him as soon as he came in so I sent one of the men ahead to notify Avessuk that I was on my way to see him.

I don't know what the bad man expected, but when I rapped

on the door he opened it at once, and stood there trembling like a leaf. I extended my hand and when he presented his, I grasped it and bore down, literally crushing it with all my strength. As I pumped his hand I looked him in the eye saying, "Avessuk, we're going to be friends. Great friends."

"Yes, friends," said Avessuk, grimacing with pain.

Well, that was it and the strange thing about it was that we did become great friends. During our stay in Shishmaref he caused no trouble for anyone and, incidentally, made Toni a couple of necklaces of the finest mammoth tooth ivory, that she still has among her souvenirs. But I never got any of the money back for his whaling associates. He had already spent it all. One look around his spacious igloo told the story. There was a cabinet phonograph, and a nice selection of recordings, a fine Lang stove, aluminum utensils, thermos bottle, Primus stove, and flashlight. There were new traps, a rifle and a shotgun with plenty of shells among the loot. Avessuk had done right well for himself.

*   *   *   *

Mrs. Whiskers Comes Home

One day, about the middle of January, 1924, we had some other visitors who caused quite a stir in the village but in a different way. They were Papa Whiskers and his wife who had come in from their home at *Abnoruk* about twenty miles distant at the mouth of the Serpentine River. She was not actually his wife but in their old age these ancient people who had lost their earlier mates had been living together and quite alone. But now Mrs. Whiskers had fallen on the ice and broken her hip and Papa had brought her home to die among her people.

Papa Whiskers came by his name honestly enough as he had snow white hair, long and stringy, and a snow white beard, as long and full as that of any Santa Claus. In fact, with his thick body, rosy cheeks, and fur clothes he looked like Santa Claus. He was what Stefansson would have called a *blonde Eskimo* for his heavy beard was quite unusual among ordinary Eskimos. Mrs. Whiskers was perhaps the oldest woman on the coast. Her hair, too, was snow white and stringy and her frail bones so dry and brittle there was no chance of them ever knitting again.

For about a week the little old woman was the center of all attraction. Everybody came to the igloo where she lay to pay her court. How her eyes sparkled at such lavish attention. Nothing like this had ever happened to her before. Never had she been so important. And Papa? He had two married sons in the village and a host of grandchildren. But nobody paid any attention to him. In a day or two, he had departed alone, to his lonely hut on the river. This was not his party.

Toni and I were busy with our school and a hundred other duties and had almost forgotten about her when one day a relative of the old one came and announced in all good cheer that Mrs. Whiskers was dead. It came as quite a shock to us for, in spite of the broken hip, the old woman a week before had been in good health and excellent spirits. No one reported her ill and nobody had requested medicine for her. We attended the burial service and prudently asked no questions. But we couldn't help suspecting that, Eskimo fashion, Mrs. Whiskers had actually and knowingly attended her own funeral (or wake) and after a week of revelry had been left unattended in an unheated igloo until life had departed the worn-out body. Eskimos have no fear of death and expect the next life to be better. So why the dread or sadness of departing?

We had read about the Eskimos' seeming cruel treatment administered to the old or crippled, especially at starving times, or when a seasonal migration was about to take place. In one example, if a person was physically unable to accompany the group, he was left with a supply of food as adequate as could be spared. If he survived the return of the group, well and good, but more often it was "farewell and so sorry."

An unwritten law also obligated close relatives to assist the hopelessly sick or in pain who preferred death to their constant agony or uselessness. Some years ago on St. Lawrence Island a woman who was dying of tuberculosis asked her brother to hang her. Unable to refuse the request, the man undertook his grim duty. He secured a stout pole about ten feet long and at one end attached a sealskin noose. Because the local missionary might interfere with the proceedings if he knew, the brother and his friends carried his ailing sister in darkness and secrecy over the hill behind the village. There the noose was placed around the woman's neck and her body raised tenderly on a sealskin blanket, while the pole was placed in an upright position. Then as strong men held the pole upright, the sealskin was pulled out from under the woman and she was strangled as she had requested. Such

measures are incomprehensible to us but the Eskimos who love
each other and have infinite faith in a better life to come,
understood.

*   *   *   *

EDDIE TAKES A BRIDE

One day a young Eskimo named Eddie paid us an official call;
we could tell it was official by his nervousness and the way he
was slicked up. After a little preliminary figiting he suddenly
blurted out, "Say, I like to marry it Grace." Feeling that his
announcement which embodied a request was entirely out of
my province, I said, "Well, Eddie, I think that you had better
ask it Grace." To which Eddie replied, "I already ask it her."

"Well, what did she say, Eddie?'

"Oh, she like it, all right!"

But there was something still troubling Eddie so I told him
I'd look into the matter and let him know later if it was all right.
Thereupon, he left after thanking me profusely for taking an
interest in his problem. It had occurred to me that someone
disapproved of the marriage and that was where the trouble lay.
Tribal organization among the Eskimos is so loose as to be
almost non-existent. Still there were incest taboos that had to be
reckoned with. In this case we found certain parties were object-
ing because, in her infancy, Grace had been fostered by a member
of Eddie's family. Because of this technicality some of the people
regarded Grace as a sister of Eddie and therefore not eligible to be
his wife. So in order to satisfy the villagers as well as ourselves
as to the propriety of such a wedding I undertook to make a
genealogical chart of the entire village. The result was somewhat
amazing. We found that, with the exception of two families who
had come from Wales, every man, woman, and child in Shishmaref was closely related. It was just one big family. And inbreed-
ing had taken its toll, apparently. Out of the population of 268,
there were several hunchbacks, one who had practically no lower
limbs, a dwarf, and at least two nitwits beside several stutterers.
But we convinced ourselves as well as the villagers that Grace and
Eddie were not too closely related for marriage and they were
given our collective blessing. No one in Shishmaref had authority
to perform a wedding so Eddie and Grace took off one morning by
dogteam for Teller where the U.S. Commissioner, who could
perform the ceremony, resided. It v.as a four or five day's trip

depending on the weather but everybody knew that at the end of
the trail all would wind up legal. Something less than a year later
Grace presented Eddie with a carbon copy that was perfectly
normal and as healthy as they come.

*   *   *   *

NAMES AND HOW THEY GOT THEM

Another thing our genealogical chart revealed was the
chaotic mess that personal names were in. Eskimos do not have
surnames if left alone. But missionaries and schoolteachers had
provided each one with a Christian name in addition to his
native name, no doubt by request. So we had in the village, George
Oolanna, Billy Atatayak and Robert Odukduduk; the chart reveal-
ing that they were brothers. Since each of these men was married
and had a number of children in school, the only thing to do was
to make each of the men's Eskimo names their children's surnames. In that case, each child's own Eskimo name became his
middle name. Since there was no mission in the vicinity, the
schoolteachers were called upon to furnish Christian names for
the newborn and each had done so according to his light. We had
in the village George Washington Koppezuruk and Abraham
Lincoln Obkanuk. There was Adam Tukoquina and his wife, Eve,
and small son, Abel. Also in one family Woodrow, Calvin and
Warren G. Nayokpuk, the latter name honoring the President
who had died a few days before our departure from Seattle.

Sometimes isolated families did the naming themselves with
curious results. We found one that had three boys named William,
Willie and Bill, respectively. In another case Tom, Tommy and
Thomas were brothers. So also were Bob and Robert. Another
family, up at Cape Espenberg, had used the Bible for their source
of names and had named one boy, Esther and another Magdalen.
For some reason or other, all the Cape Espenberg natives that we
knew had taken the name *Barr* as a surname. Thus we had
Sublook Barr, Mukkiaktuk Barr, Adrian Barr and Peter Kouglook
Barr. We discouraged this practice, however, feeling that the
picturesque and meaningful native names should be preserved.

We had hardly gotten settled in Shishmaref when we began
being asked to name babies. And I might say right here that
Eskimo babies are born all around the calendar just like they are
anywhere else. I recall reading a book about Eskimos in which the
author stated that Eskimos have a *rutting season* like animals

each spring with the result that the children are all born about the same time. Of course, this was rubbish.

We decided to let the missionaries give Biblical names if they so desired. We didn't want to burden any little Eskimo with the name of a President or some famous man with the hidden implication that he must live up to it, so we just gave them the names of our friends back home with no strings attached.

The giving of Eskimo names was the parents' business but the translation of a few of them might give some insight into the Eskimo's sense of humor. For instance a name like *Pootoogoluk* means "sore toe"; *Kazeedluk* "skinless"; *"Taokpuk* "big sneeze"; *Kioutalluk* "no spoon"; *Ak-kitaluk* "no mittens"; *Azgayuk* "star fish." One man named *Odukduduk,* meaning "taken back," acquired his name when, as a child he had been given away by his mother and then taken back. Other Eskimo names in the village meant liver, kidney, stranger, ptarmigan and bullet. It is little wonder that they asked for Christian names.

In some villages, we learned, Christian names were not come by so easily. We once asked a native from Point Hope what his name was. He replied "Which one you want? My Eskimo name or my *white fox* name?" We found that a missionary up there had been in the practice of charging a white fox pelt for a Christening. In their inimitable way the Eskimos were registering a sly protest.

Chapter V

OUR SCHOOL AGAIN

As the school supplies, dribbling in by dogteam from Wales, began to accumulate, we gradually developed into a conventional school. However, it was clear that mere book learning would have little value to these people in their present situation. It did make it possible for them to write notes and letters to their friends. It helped them to read and understand the Bible and this was important to them. But best of all, it made it possible for them to read the mail-order catalogs and to send out orders. This alone was worth the cost and the effort, for to a great extent, it freed them from the traders, who in many instances cruelly overcharged them for necessities.

We wanted to have some type of handwork at least once a week but there was no shop and the schoolroom designed for about thirty pupils was accommodating more than sixty. Twice a week we held a barbering class in which the older boys clipped each other's hair and that of the smaller boys. This improved the appearance of the boys remarkably, for the ordinary Eskimo tonsure consists of combing the hair down over the forehead, holding a board under the locks, and chopping them off with a butcher knife. This resulted in bangs which reached the eyebrows. Now, for the first time, our boys were showing foreheads. I was wearing my own hair pompadour at the time and it was not long before the older boys began requesting vaseline. In no time most of them were combing their hair straight back and their wild aspects disappeared.

Toni had had her hair bobbed, Buster Brown style, for the first time in Ketchikan . . . one of the new freedoms enjoyed in Alaska but still frowned upon stateside as a suitable coiffure for schoolteachers. Now that we had improved the appearance of the boys we thought that bobbing would do as much for the girls. But no soap! They would not part with their braids however much they were imbedded with eider down and reindeer hair. Politely they said with unanimity, "Fine for white woman. No good for Eskimo!"

We had noticed that practically no commercial ivory carving was being done in the village whereas on the Diomedes and on King Island and at Wales, ivory carving was second only to hunting and trapping as a means of providing those most desirable white man's dollars. We found that the reason was due to Shishmaref's being off the beaten track and seldom visited by any craft. There was no demand for curios or souvenirs so the natives made none. Never-the-less we believed that such items could be made locally and sold in Nome or even Seattle. So we started an ivory-carving class. The tools were simple enough. All one needed to get into business was a hacksaw, a drill, some rasps and files and a home-made gouge. Beyond these, a supply of sandpaper and some brass polish finished the kit. Ivory was easy to come by even though these people were not walrus hunters. Dead walruses occasionally drifted ashore from which the tusks and teeth were always salvaged and beautifully-colored fossil ivory could be found on the beach after every storm. This consisted of loose walrus teeth and tusks and the tusks and teeth of the extinct mammoth. The boys took to carving like it was a second nature and soon were turning out strings of beads, bracelets, figurines, paper knives and a host of other small items. Large pieces became cribbage boards which had a ready market in Nome, or umbrella handles, gavels etc. Our boys could look at a picture of something in a book or catalog and reproduce it in three dimensions with uncanny precision. One boy made a pair of ivory scissors that could cut paper; another made an ivory twist bit with which he could drill wood. They made steel gravers from worn-out three-cornered files and engraved many of their carvings with hunting scenes or the landscapes of their environment. Altogether, it was a most successful undertaking since the village men became interested also, and soon ivory carving had regained the importance it had enjoyed in former years when ivory was the iron of the Eskimo and they fashioned it into harpoon heads and hundreds of other items of daily use.

Of course, we couldn't expect the girls to carve ivory. That was a masculine occupation. Eskimos observe a division of labor and there is no crossing the line in the primitive society. Lately there are some departures but they are frowned upon. Men provide the meat; women process it. Men bring in the hides; women work them up. Men catch the fish; women dry them. (Here, tomcod jigging is an exception) Men carve; women sew.

We had noticed that none of these women made baskets. In other villages basketry was an important craft and baskets were much in use. But here, bentwood boxes made of driftwood, and bags and pouches made of sealskin or gut took the place of baskets. It was not for the lack of basket material that no baskets were made for on the sand dunes near the village grew a wild rye, tall and tough, ideal for basket-making.

Toni had made coiled baskets of raffia, so it was no trick to substitute wild rye for raffia. She started the class and it was soon evident that these girls needed no teacher. Only a leader. Without exception, their nimble fingers were soon turning out perfect specimens, decorated with geometric designs of their own choosing. Here, again, it was simply a case of re-introducing an age-old craft that had been abandoned for lack of need or incentive. The skill and dexterity were innate; there was needed only a reason for putting it work and the tourist market provided that.

Out in the coal shed there was a portable forge. We had no smithing coal but we got along very well on Utah nut coal that we used for heating. There was also an anvil and some blacksmith tools so we started a class in iron working. We had little good steel to work with but there was a cache of old files and rasps, some gun barrels, etc. It was always well below zero in the coal shed but with the heat from the forge to keep their hands warm the boys could work. We made knives mostly. First we would draw the temper from the files so we could shape the blade and tang and drill holes through which the handles could be riveted on. Then we would re-temper the blades by re-heating and immersion in water so that they could be hard enough to hold an edge but not fly to pieces if used for chopping at 30 or 40 degrees below zero. That was the acid test, for of all the commercial knives used in the area only one could pass. This was an English butcher knife known throughout the Arctic as a *Willson knife*. To achieve the temper of a *Willson knife* was every boy's dream.

For handles, we used walrus ivory or reindeer antler. After the handles had been riveted on, the boys spent hours polishing the blades, until they shone like mirrors. None of these knives were ever offered for sale since each boy seemed to regard his knife as something too personal ever to be parted with.

Chapter VI

DOCTORING

One of the things that had concerned us somewhat was our diet. We knew the Eskimos were not subject to scurvy or beriberi since they ate a great deal of raw food. This was not only fish, but great quantities of willow leaves and fernweed flowers, besides uncookd cranberries, cloudberries and *empetrum nigrum* berries. But we didn't like our fish raw or berries, flowers and leaves preserved in seal oil. In our grocery list, we had included lime juice, sauerkraut, potatoes and onions to be our anti-scorbutics. But the lime juice had frozen and broken its bottles at Wales. The potatoes and onions could not be transported over the trail without freezing so they had been disposed of where they were. That left the sauerkraut which finally got to us and was delicious, frozen. But in the meantime Toni had developed a batch of boils on her sitdown. These were not ordinary boils that come to a head eventually. On the contrary, they were deep-seated, purplish blue swellings that got as large as hens' eggs. We suspected they were the result of a diet deficiency but their cause was purely academic. The problem was how to get rid of them.

In our medicine chest, we had a surgeon's scalpel but Toni didn't have the nerve to let me use it. I might add that neither did I, yet there was no other course. We were on our own. Our medical supplies included a small quantity of grain alcohol. I suggested to Toni that I make her a drink to help fortify her for the operation, to which she consented in a weak moment. Having grown up in a prohibition era we knew little or nothing about alcohol. The cocktail I produced was a tumbler half of grain alcohol and half of canned grape juice. Toni drained the glass and I sat back to await results while sterilizing the scalpel on the kitchen stove. They were not long in coming. Toni was soon quite drunk but too pugnacious to let me operate. I had difficulty in holding her down let alone use the scalpel. Then a terrifying change took place in her. Her eyes took on the appearance of those of a hunted animal and her voice changed to the harsh cracking of an insane person. Finally she collapsed and I steeled myself to plunge the knife in. The pressure within the boils must have been terrific as the corrupt contents spurted out with great force, nearly a cupful to the boil. The operation left us both shaken, but the next morning Toni was much better, except for the hangover, and she was never seriously troubled thereafter.

There is this to be said about my medical career at Shishmaref. Whenever I was called, it was an emergency. There was Billy Atatayak's boy with a high fever and his right leg drawn up with the knee under his chin, too sore to touch above the right groin. It looked like appendicitis but that was one operation I wouldn't attempt. I remembered a roommate at college who had chronic appendicitis and had to take olive oil every day. Now, we had a gallon of olive oil that our Seattle grocery mentor had said we would need and up to now hadn't touched. Billy's boy got it, cup by cup, and somehow he recovered. Maybe it helped, maybe it didn't, but we chalked it up as another victory for medical science.

One dark night we were awakened by someone standing beside our bed imploring us to get up. We didn't have a lock on the door and no watchdog, either, so it was nothing unusual to expect from Eskimos who don't even knock. It was Peter Barr telling us his baby was "bad sick, maybe dead already."

Peter's baby was something special with us for she was the first child in Shishmaref that we had named and we certainly wanted little Dolores to live if there was a chance. I dressed and followed Peter across the village to his igloo. The baby lay on the floor in the small room filled with relatives and all the friends of the family who could crowd in. What little air there was, was thick enough to cut and steaming hot. The baby had a high fever and its pulse was so weak you could hardly find it. It looked like pneumonia.

The first thing I did was run everybody out of the igloo but Peter and his wife. Then I lit out for home to take a look at the book.

I knew I had to build up that pulse and the book said quinine would do it. But it also said you couldn't prescribe quinine for an infant. I took out one of the tablets and looked at it. If this is a dose for an adult, about half a tablet should be about right for a child, I thought, and cut it in two. Now, I thought, if this is the proper dose for a child, half of it ought to be about right for an infant. I cut the tablet again and, taking the quarter dose, ran back to Peter's igloo. The tablet administered, we sat back to await results. Before long I noticed a slight quickening of the pulse. That was gratifying. A little later the pulse was strong and normal. I felt good. Now, if it would just keep that way. But no, a few minutes later the pulse was pounding at a terrific clip. I knew it couldn't last. I must find something to slow it down again.

Back I raced to our cottage and out came the medical book. Soon I found what we needed—Dover's powder. But again the book said it was not for infants. Using my formula for quinine, x divided by 4, x being the adult dosage, I quartered the tablet and rushed back to the igloo. There was barely time but the dose had the desired affect. The heart slowed down and the child slept. By morning the crisis had passed and Dolores had survived both the malady and the treatment. She grew into a healthy though not beautiful child.

It was my treatment for heart attack on which my professional standing in the community actually rested. We had observed that whenever they brought in a beluga whale they all went on a *muktuk* binge and shortly thereafter I would have a number of heart attack cases. In case you don't know, muktuk is the whale's skin and the attached layer of blubber. From a beluga, or white whale, the muktuk cut into squares looks like New York ice cream. First there is a punky layer of white. Beneath this is a thinner layer of black which is the skin. Beneath this is a third, thick layer of pale pink blubber, or fat. Eaten frozen, it has a not unpleasant taste, resembling coconut meat, but to Eskimos it is ambrosia. They gorge themselves on it at every opportunity.

I gathered that the so-called heart attack was only a palpitation brought on by gas on the stomach. So our remedy was soda water. Whenever we saw a whale coming up the beach we went home and made up five gallons of soda water—not the carbonated water beverage commonly referred to as soda water but ordinary branch water and bicarbonate. To this, by means of deception, we added a little cake coloring to give it an attractive pink color. I don't think they ever caught on but the remedy always gave instant relief to the accompaniment of frequent burps which are always well-received in Eskimo society.

I have often wished that I had had some medical training before going up there for if I had I am sure I could have made a few interesting contributions to medical literature. The Eskimos had a number of odd and unusual maladies and odder treatments. They had, for instance, a skin disease that gradually destroyed the pigment. They had boils that developed amazingly fast and healed even faster. Their ability to heal rapidly was almost unbelievable. I recall a trapper who came in with a finger cut to the bone. He had wrapped it in a piece of sealgut and when he came to me the wound was gaping, the bone exposed and skin snow white. I put on an antiseptic dressing, pulled the wound together as best I could, wrapped it up and told the patient to come in to have it re-dressed every day. He did this a couple times then he left and didn't show up for a week. I jumped him the next time I saw him and hauled him in, expecting the worst. But what I saw when the bandage was removed, was a finger completely healed.

Then there was the old woman who had a huge abscess on her hip. Each winter we would open it, drain off a cup of pus and assorted fragments of bone, and she would be good for another year. We came to the conclusion that the magic elixir of life that kept them going was the pint or so of seal oil they drank every day. What else?

The most mysterious of the common Eskimo maladies was one that they treated themselves. Eskimos have doctors, usually if not always, women known as *feelers*. These women seem to have very sensitive fingers with which they explore one's anatomy and seek out the seat of the trouble. If one would have a headache, the feeler would go over the scalp until she found the spot. She would then insert a tiny blade and out would spurt air or some kind of gas under pressure. The headache would thereupon subside. These same women treated snowblindness by surgery. The treatment consisted of pinching up the skin between the eyes, driving the knife through it and draining off the "bad blood." This may have speeded up recovery, at least they thought it did.

In dentistry, my professional skill was no better than my knowledge of medicine. Our dental equipment consisted of a pair each of upper and lower forceps and a bottle of tooth drops. Since I was never called upon to make a bridge or a set of dentures or even fill a cavity, they were perhaps all I needed. But occasionally someone would want an aching tooth extracted and we had to accommodate.

My constant fear was that I might break a tooth off, thereby leaving my patient worse off than ever since I had no anesthetics and less knowledge of how to remove a root. So I dared not rock the tooth, or so I thought. My procedure was to place the patient flat on his back on the living room couch. I then cupped my left hand across his forehead and sometimes my knee on his chest.

Then I took a firm grip on the tooth with the forceps and literally horsed it out with a straight, steady pull. My smiling patients always got the tooth for a souvenir.

What the Shishmaref natives may have lacked in medical science they easily made up for in common sense. They may have discounted the germ theory of disease but they certainly knew that some diseases are carried and spread by man and by man alone. The climate itself was enough to destroy any germ not enjoying the artificial climate of its host so these people were free of most contagious diseases so long as they were left alone. A good example was the so-called *cheechako cold* that nobody ever caught until the first boat of the season arrived. Then everybody got it.

In 1918 when the Spanish influenza was ravaging the world it came to Alaska, too, and took its toll of death, particularly among the native peoples. Like wildfire it spread from Ketchikan to Nome and on to Wales where it took the lives of five out of every seven people. By mukluk telegraph the Shishmaref natives learned of the marching death and prepared to deal with it. They set up a barricade across the trail at the southwest end of their island and manned it day and night. Not one traveler, white or Eskimo, was allowed to approach, even the barricade, closer than hailing distance. The result was that the influenza never got a foot farther than the Shishmaref barricade in its march over the world. A single band of Eskimos armed with nothing more than common sense, rifles, and determination saved not only themselves but everybody north of them. Was there ever another such event in the annals of medical history?

Chapter VII

OUR POLYGAMIST

Winter is the social season for the Eskimos. The brief summer is a time of prodigous labor, with the populace scattered in little camps over an immense coastal expanse with friends pretty much out of communication with each other. But the fierce winter drives them back to the shelter of their dugout habitations in compact villages. Now the women can get together to exchange news and to catch up on the latest scandal and gossip.

The practice is to congregate in little parties in someone's igloo, there to sew skin garments, make mukluks, and to gossip. It was an occasion like this that one day found half a dozen women arriving at the spacious Tocktoo igloo. Tocktoo, a former *shaman,* or medicine man, was the only polygamist in town. Formerly polygamy had been a common Eskimo practice but now, women being in short supply, most men were content to possess only one. Tocktoo had married his first wife for her beauty and she was referred to in the village as Mrs. Tocktoo number one. Sometime later he took another wife; this one for her brains. She, of course, was known as Mrs. Tocktoo number two. On this particular day no one was home but number two. And beside her on the floor where she sewed was a 30-30 caliber rifle. Asked the meaning of this, the woman with brains told her story. When she and Tocktoo had married there was no trouble and no gossip. Both she and Mrs. Tocktoo number one had reared large families in the same house. No trouble. Then the missionaries came and preached to the people. It was not right, they said, for a man to have two wives. He must give up one of them. Since that time every winter when the villagers held services the polygamy question would come up, again and again. Now, said number two, Tocktoo could stand the gossip no longer. He was going to give up one of his wives and she knew it would be her. So, she told her guests, rather than to be thrown out, she was going to kill Tocktoo when he came home. That explained the presence of the rifle.

The good wives tarried, naturally, to see the excitement. It was not long in coming. A noise was heard at the stormshed door and presently there was a clatter just outside the inner door. Mrs. Tocktoo number two picked up the rifle, cocked it, and held it in readiness. The door opened and in strode Tocktoo. The woman aimed and fired. Tocktoo staggered and clapped his hand over his forehead as blood streamed down over his face. Then he uttered a few magic words, wiped the blood from his forehead, came in and sat down without even reproaching his wife. The awestricken guests, never having heard of blank cartridges, departed precipitiously to spread the electrifying news that Tocktoo had regained his supernatural power. One of them burst into our house with the news only minutes after the shot was fired. We received the news with all due respect but as soon as our informant left I went out to have a look before it was too late. Quietly I entered Tocktoo's stormshed and looked around. Just as I had suspected, there lay a freshly-killed seal. I put my hand inside the body cavity. It was still warm, and the blood had not congealed. I left immediately and kept my discovery to myself. Thereafter nobody brought up the subject of Tocktoo's other wife and sofar as I know the woman with brains lived happily ever after.

*   *   *   *

OTHER SHAMANS

The Tocktoo episode brought out a whole rash of tales of shamanism of bygone days and we gathered that these conjurers were pretty foxy in their day, living by their wits and taking advantage of the incredulity and superstitions of their fellows. They were pretty generally hated and feared, too, for the shamans had them believing that no matter what the people did to them, they'd come back and get even. One, however, was so tyrannical they killed him, anyway. And then to make sure that he'd never come back they cut off all his fingers and toes, sewed them in his stomach and burned the entire body. That one never came back.

Another shaman, in order to demonstrate to the people that he still had his power, invited everybody to see him perform his magic in the sand dunes southwest of the village. At this place he had four fires burning at the corners of a square in which he sat with his drum. As the fires burned fiercely from seal oil that had been poured on, the shaman beat his drum and chanted. The assemblage then saw him apparently getting smaller and smaller until he disappeared entirely. They had been cautioned not to go near the fires but to return home and reassemble in four days at which time the shaman would reappear.

At the appointed time everybody in the village went back to the place and sat down on the dunes to await the miraculous reappearance. Time passed but nothing happened. At length, some of the men went down to the place where the fires had burned and began poking around. Some thought the old shaman might have burned up and if so, there should be some charred bones around. Then one of the men discovered what appeared to be the top of a willow basket buried in the sand between the burned out fires. A little excavating soon revealed that it was, indeed, a large basket. And doubled up within it was the body of the shaman. By an ingenious arrangement, the shaman had let himself down into the basket while the fires had dried and sifted sand over the cover. Apparently he had suffered a heart attack and died because of the cramped position. At any rate, it was a good idea that just didn't pan out.

The Eskimos told us that, actually, the shamans were simply the agents of the devil who ruled their country until white prospectors arrived around 1900. Shortly after gold was discovered on the Nome beach, white men poured into the country by the thousands and explored every inch of the adjacent country. One such prospector travelling with an Eskimo companion decided to spend the night in a deserted igloo. The Eskimo cautioned him against it, however, saying that this igloo was taboo as it was a favorite lodging place of the devil. The white man laughed off the Eskimos' admonition and moved in. But that night a commotion was heard outside and the Eskimo fell to the floor in a faint. The prospector threw a robe over him, then opened the door. In walked the devil and there insued a terrific battle. The Eskimo recovered enough to lift the edge of the robe and watch the fight. The devil was lightning fast and tricky. Moreover, he was a hard as dried leather but the white man was harder and drier and trickier. The devil was finally beaten so bad, that he took to his heels and never came back. And when he left all the shamans in Alaska lost their power. Even the skull that lay between the whale jawbones just north of town quit talking to passersby and hasn't said a word since. So it is little wonder that when Tocktoo got his power back it was a noteworthy event. There hadn't been a worthwhile shaman around for twenty years.

Chapter VIII

OUR GUESTS, WINTER EVENTS AND ACTIVITIES

We were too occupied with teaching and other duties to have any afternoon visitors but there never was an evening that didn't find our living room crowded. Not that we were so popular, but we had the most to offer. In the first place, heated with good old Government coal, it was the warmest place in town. Besides, we had a phonograph and a fair assortment of records and all Eskimos are born music lovers. Then we had a large assortment of National Geographic magazines over which they would pore endlessly. Even though they couldn't read, many of the adults would find the illustrations thought-provoking and from their questions we got an inkling of what they thought of the rest of the world. To this little band, their world was the Seward Peninsula. The rest of the world was a similar piece of land, infinitely far distant and as unattainable as the moon. It was a land that, in their wildest dreams, they never expected to see. They knew practically every inhabitant of Seward Peninsula; they expected us to know personally every person in the world we had come from. For example, they would point to the picture of a Hottentot or an Igorote in a magazine and ask us what his name was. Also, why didn't he wear any clothes? And why are some white people black? It was wearying but not entirely onesided. For we asked questions, too, that must have seemed quite as stupid. But they never let on, and spent endless hours instructing us on how to live in their land and avoid its perils. They entertained us with their folklore and tales which we carefully put down against the day when we could have them published. For we had the feeling that with the changing times we were sitting in on the end of an era and things that were not written down would soon be lost forever.

Our guests seemed to feel it would be impolite to get up and leave without permission so it became our duty about nine o'clock each evening to announce that it was time to go home whereupon everyone would get up (they always sat on the floor), thank us profusely and leave.

This business of sitting on the floor was not necessarily due

to our lack of chairs, although it could have been. We couldn't
have seated half a dozen guests on chairs but they wouldn't have
used them, anyway. These people habitually sat at work or at
rest, not squatting on their haunches like Indians, but flat on
their sitdowns with feet extended. They got so they could bend
only at right angles, and chairs were a hardship. Women, working
on their feet cutting up fish or seal, habitually bend at the waist,
never at the knees, and in old age often would be seen assuming
the position just for a rest.

Men carved ivory or split wood sitting down. They rode their
kayaks in the same position and women sat on the floor to sew or
prepare meals. Eskimo food was served on the floor from low
tables and people ate sitting with their feet outstretched. But a
change was already taking place. We noticed that in several
households when white man's food was served it was eaten from
conventional tables at which the diners sat on benches.

Toni and I rarely made social calls unless it was to see a new
baby or greet a friend who had just returned to the village from a
trip. Few of the women spoke English and nobody had so much
as a chair in the way of furniture so we imagined our visits would
be more a source of embarrassment than an honor. Besides, they
could always visit us. But on medical calls or visits to trade for a
piece of ivory or a bag or eiderdown we got to see the inside of
everyone's igloo often enough.

*   *   *   *

HARD WATER

All winter the coming of Saturday offered the pleasant
diversion of ice-cutting since ice was the only source of water for
the entire community. Just beyond the village were several
brackish ponds that were the unpromising source of usable ice.
However, in the process of freezing, the salt was eliminated to
a great extent, and the ice was better than would be reasonably
expected. When the first ice got a foot or more in thickness, the
crop would be cut and that, not immediately required, would be
stacked at the edge of the pond like cordwood. Then the ponds
would refill from beneath and in a few days the process could
be repeated. After three or four crops had been harvested the
ponds would suddenly go dry and no more water would appear
before spring.

Ice-cutting was the chore of adolescent boys and they worked at it cheerfully with considerable vigor. But suddenly in the midst of their work, the saws and tongs would be dropped and all of the boys would sit down to put on their skates. Such skates as theirs would not be found any place else in the world. Manufactured skates could not be used since they could not be fastened to the soft sole of a winter mukluk. So the Eskimos made their own. Pieces of spruce driftwood the length and width of the mukluk sole would be carved roughly into the form of a round-bottomed boat. Then slots were sawed into these wooden pieces to receive the blades which were held in place by bone or ivory pegs. The blades were made of skeletal whalebone or short lengths of iron sledge shoes. In either case they served the purpose. These odd skates were equipped with sealskin thongs by which they were lashed to the mukluks. The boys would skate recklessly and with enjoyment for about fifteen minutes and then stop as suddenly as they had begun and resume the ice-cutting.

After the ice had been harvested from all the ponds, and stacked, it was hauled home in small sleds as needed. Sometimes near the end of the winter this supply could be supplemented by glacier or river ice which from time to time rode the sea ice as the pack moved before the village. These chunks could be distinguished easily from the salt ice by color and clarity, the fresh ice appearing blue against the yellowish ice of the sea. If too large for one man to handle, a group would go out, lasso the berg and tow it shoreward, where it would be grounded and could be cut up as needed.

* * * *

OUR FIRE

The fact that the entire village's supply of water was in the form of ice hadn't concerned us too much until the day our house caught fire. It had been my practice to run over to the house every recess to check on the fires which of necessity must be kept burning day and night. Approaching the entrance that day I saw a thin wisp of white smoke issuing from above the stormshed door. Dashing up the steps and opening this, I found flames licking around the top of the inner door. Opening this I was met with a blast of smoke, chemicals, and super-heated air that almost sent me reeling back. Inside through the smoke I saw fire on the kitchen partition, also. With a bucket of dishwater, I drenched both places and the fire was out. But now the alarm had been given and people were running up from all directions with their pitiful offerings of water. Nobody had more than a quart in which several small chunks of ice were floating but they sloshed it on in good community spirit and felt good for having helped save our home.

Apparently a downdraft of wind had blown a spark out of our kitchen stove which landed in a nearby box of kindling wood and set it afire. But fortunately a Pyrene fire extinguisher hung just above it. When the fire was hot enough it melted the solder of the extinguisher, spilling its contents where it was most needed. It didn't put out the fire but certainly retarded it. The fire had licked the paint from walls and ceilings, that was about all. What had saved our home was caulking around the windows and doors. For the fire had burned until it had used up the oxygen contained in the house and was dying in its own smoke when I arrived.

We were congratulating ourselves on our narrow escape from a winter in an igloo when we happened to recall that the attic held some $5000 worth of white fox pelts belonging to the natives. We got them out in the light where we found the smoke had converted the whole lot to artificial blues. For the moment we were sick, as it was apparent the natives had sustained a terrific loss that we felt responsible for. But again we were lucky. At the suggestion of one of the villagers we purchased a 100 pound sack of yellow cornmeal which is used in the village for dog feed. This we dumped into a tub and set some boys to work cleaning the pelts at twenty-five cents each. We were amazed at the results they got. For the cornmeal not only took off the smoke but also the oil in the furs, leaving them whiter and fluffier than before. And when the furs were later sold on the Seattle Fur Exchange we found that their superior quality and handling had brought premium prices.

Chapter IX

MIRAGES AND OTHER
PHENOMENA

One would not expect to find much of aesthetic value in a flat tundra land adjoining a frozen sea yet we found beauty in a hundred forms and more often in the depths of winter than summer. The rising of the December sun which occurs about eleven a.m. in these latitudes is of breathtaking grandeur. At this time of year the sun describes a low arc just above the skyline, consequently the sunrise or period when the sun is immediately beneath the horizon or just peeping over is necessarily of longer duration than it would be in lower latitudes. On such occasions the distant panorama and narrow stratum of clouds lying just above the horizon assumes a rich blueblack tone. There is a band of reddish orange sky lying above the cloud which, as it merges with the deep blue of the heavens, creates a brilliant green. The foreground is still wrapped in sombre black and the tall poles of the caches, the stacks of driftwood and the igloos stand out in silhouette against the colored backdrop. Animation of the scene comes from purplish smoke rising from the igloos and the twinkling of a myriad silver stars not yet erased by the coming brief day.

Fortunately for dwellers in the Arctic the sun is not the only source of light for in December the sun has so little intensity that only by facing it would you know it was there and to the west the stars are still twinkling. But if there happens to be a full moon, then the night is brighter than the day. Reflected by the ice and snow and aided by countless stars and often by the aurora, the moon casts shadows on the snow, objects a mile away are easily recognized and even hunting is not impossible.

Because of minute ice crystals in the otherwise clear atmosphere we saw phenomena almost daily that we had never seen at home in the misty Puget Sound country. There were solar and lunar halos, sometimes doubled and spoked with sundogs at the intersections. We saw fog bows, light pillars, mirages and auroras of many types, some quite terrifying which we will describe shortly.

But first the mirages. These were best from November through March on the coldest, clearest and stillest days. This

curious optical effect of elevation, distortion, and inversion of
distant objects was principally noticed in its distortion of mountains but affected distant ships and the moon as well. Ordinarily
only Ear mountain was visible from the village but if the conditions for mirage were right then mountains would spring up as if
by magic and form an unbroken chain from east to southwest
along the entire expanse of the mainland. Kougarok mountain 40
miles east, Nuluk and Potato mountains 50 to 60 miles away and
even Wales mountain 75 miles distant, airline, would rise up to
appear at least 5000 feet in elevation whereas none were more
than half of that. As you watched them the rounded summits
would stretch upwards as if pulled by invisible hands until they
appeared lofty and sharp-pointed. Then the narrow peaks would
suddenly widen, the mountains now appearing as mesas. In a
few moments these mesas would send out thin cornices which
soon would join other cornices to form a chain of natural
bridges. But at other times the mountains would retain their
peaks while a second range of identical mountains would form,
upside down, above them, peak to peak, reminiscent of a
gigantic balancing act.

Even the moon is not immune to these optical distortions
for as it rises and sets through the low lying atmospheric stratum
it presents the most unbelievable forms. Usually it appears as a
Japanese lantern twice as tall as it is broad, blood red in color,
slightly squared at top and bottom and not infrequently broken
into horizontal segments lying directly above each other with
equal spaces intervening. Other times it appears pumpkin-like
with small bites taken from equi-distant points on its edge. Once
we saw a double moon rise, the lower one only half exposed above
the horizon. It looked like the head and shoulders of some colossal
being gazing over the edge of the world. While we looked, the neck
stretched and finally snapped with head floating free above the
shoulders. As the moon rose above the miraging stratum it assumed the characteristic silvery brilliancy and the red shoulders
withdrew below the horizon.

Spring mirages were common up until the time when the ice
on the ocean broke up and drifted northward early in July. During
this time objects scarcely a mile distant were stretched upward
until a small hummock would appear to be a good-sized hill, and
to seaward there sometimes appeared a wall of ice suggesting the
terminus of a glacier discharging into the sea or again as the high

bank of another land suddenly thrust up in the ocean. Sometimes *open water* is seen at these times causing the inhabitants to believe there will be an early break-up but upon investigation, these patches of open water are found to be non-existent or at least miles beyond the place where they were seen.

Following the break-up and again just before the freeze-up, approaching vessels will be seen, but the phantom ship never arrives. It is probably nothing more than a chunk of discolored ice to which the mirage had added masts and sails or it might be only a humble kayak, magnified and distorted until it looked like a schooner. But sometimes real ships are miraged. We remember one that we watched as it sailed away to the north. Then suddenly it was inverted, and we watched it sail out of sight on the tip of its mast. We often wondered what the Eskimos thought of all this since they had no scientific information to help explain it. But it was an old story with them and did no real harm so they took it in their stride, not asking an explanation.

After the first of October and until the end of March the aurora borealis could be witnessed almost every night. So long as cold weather continued nothing seemed to interfere with the nightly displays except the return of the sun. The commonest form of the aurora at Shishmaref was an arc of pale, colorless light that appeared on the northern horizon. This arc varied in both heighth and width, it being low and narrow in a dead calm. At times the crown was double, one appearing above the other and rarely, a smaller crown would appear to the left of the first, forming a double arch. When the wind was high the arch would rise then seem to break into segments which would float away in the sky.

But there were time when we witnessed appalling displays that filled the entire heavens with colored draperies which were so low and dense they threatened to crush us into the frozen earth. At these times a muffled cracking noise could be heard distinctly by everyone and the small Eskimo boys would band together and race about the tundra imitating the sounds they heard. These spectacular displays gave off the odor of ozone, somewhat like the smell of fresh blood and one could feel slight electric shocks or tickling about the ears. Again we noticed the Eskimos attached no superstition to the aurora, noting only the increased displays foretold colder weather and northerly winds.

Another phenomenon that we hadn't expected and which

gave us some uneasy moments for a time was the local earth-quake. After a period of several months of sub-zero weather the earth would literally crack open with a roar, shaking any house or igloo that happened to be nearby. Fissures from four to six inches wide would appear that could be traced several hundred feet. These quakes happened so frequently that the natives took no notice of them unless one occurred directly under a row of igloos at which time it would send the occupants scurrying outside like scared rabbits. Small ponds, too, would sometimes freeze into a convex surface and then explode at the center like a volcano, scattering chunks of ice in all directions and producing a miniature crater exposing dry mud at the bottom. We often heard a sound like thunder or distant cannonading to seaward but the natives explained that this was a similar cracking of the sea ice which would be from four to five feet thick at this time.

During the long freeze-up it was difficult for us to get suffi-cient exercise. We began taking long walks on the beach each day at first bucking the wind as long as we could take it, then turning back and allowing the wind to blow us home. We soon found this wasn't enough. So we reversed the procedure and, going with the wind, allowed it to push us much farther than we would have bucked it, then battled our way against it back to the village. Sometimes we were barely able to make it. The force of the arctic gale as well as the steadiness of the winter winds was almost beyond belief but since we had no anemometer we will never know what their velocity was. At times we could actually lean against it and be held up. Toni learned its strength the hard way. One day as school was being dismissed she noticed a small boy standing in the trail, crying. A group of sympathetic play-mates were standing by and watching something on the tundra which she recognized as his cap. She thereupon took after it and soon had it in her hand. But when she tried to return with it, she couldn't take a step against the wind. Her only recourse was to lie down and crawl from niggerhead to niggerhead until she came into the lee of the coal shed where, with the protection afforded, she was able to regain the trail. I recall my own experience when I tried to round the same shed with four empty coal hods. The wind which was gusty that day caught them suddenly like they were sails and I was lifted up and thrown against the shed so hard I nearly broke my hip and was laid up for several days.

Chapter X

RETURN OF THE SUN

When April finally arrived a definite change took place in the life of the village. It could not exactly be called spring although the sun now had considerable warmth and the days were almost without end. But the sea ice was intact and snow still covered the tundra. What changed village life was the closing of the trapping season and, one might say, the opening of the travelling season. For now the trappers came home with their traps and the season's catch to tarry with their families a few days and then take off on the annual trading trip.

These trading trips were perhaps entirely unnecessary from a financial point of view, but socially, well that was something else again. The trapper at best could make only a dollar or two more on his furs at Deering, Kotzebue or even Nome than he could from local traders, and besides would have to freight his goods home. But one would get nowhere trying to point this out to the trapper. To him this seasonal jaunt was purely for social purposes and worked wonders with his ego. An Eskimo with a couple dozen fox pelts to barter was a man of importance in those days. A few miles from his destination he would stop, dress up in his best parka and mukluks, put on his fancy mittens, and then dash into town like a visiting potentate. If far enough from home to get away with it he might even boast of his wealth and importance at home. He would be wined and dined, so to speak, by the traders and would prolong his trading to exact the utmost in hospitality and entertainment, knowing full well that as soon as the furs were sold, the party would be over and he would be obliged to return home and again face the realities of life.

There were other travelers who came into the village or passed through on some mission or other during April and May which was the ideal time for travelling by dogteam. We had a visit from the Reverend Mr. Dahle, Lutheran missionary at Teller Mission who baptized all the children born since his last visit or the last visit of some other itinerant priest or preacher. The Eskimos enjoyed ceremony and had their children baptized as often as opportunity arrived, regardless the denomination. I recall one beaming father who remarked to me after Dahle's visit, "Well, all my kits Lutheran, now. Last year him all Catholic!"

All visitors were welcome to us and if white, were domiciled with us, the Eskimos preferring to put up with the villagers among whom they always had personal friends or relatives. Our guests included missionaries, school officials, fur buyers, game wardens, or a U.S. Marshal. Sometimes a writer or scientist or Lomen reindeer man might stop by, or even a Kougarok miner looking for dog feed. They added up to about a dozen a year and through them we received letters and news that otherwise would have had to wait until the opening of navigation in July. And it was through them that we were able to mail letters home from time to time or to send an order for supplies in to Nome that otherwise would have had to wait until the break-up.

We closed school at the end of April, almost by request, as the villagers were anxious to move out to their *oogruk* camps. Everybody got out of his igloo as soon as possible and pitched tents in the vicinity until ready to take off for the permanent summer camp.

If I were to assign a particular occupation to the Shishmaref people I would have to say that they were primarily oogruk hunters, for in spite of the value of the furs they trap, or their reindeer herds, the oogruk represents the greater value to their economy. This huge bearded hair seal furnishes dried meat for the winter, oil which is the butter of the land, being superior in flavor to walrus or ordinary seal oil, mukluk soles, and lashing which takes the place of rope and other cordage in these latitudes. Any surplus hides could be sold for $10 each and the lashing at 75¢ per pound.

About the first of May the oogruk appear off Shishmaref heading north with the moving ice pack. In order to intercept the herd at as many points as possible, the natives spread out along the beach for a hundred miles or so in little bands spaced a mile or so apart. I doubt that these groups are ever out of hailing distance of each other, otherwise the famous *mukluk telegraph* wouldn't work as it does. If the wind is from the north the hunters venture out to the edge of the stationary ice to get to the moving floe which may be as much as thirty miles offshore. The dogs pull large low native-designed sledges known locally as *oogruk sleds*. The oogruk may weigh as much as 500 pounds so these low sledges are built to facilitate loading and to stand up under heavy loading.

Hunting on the ice may be as prosaic as a Sunday School

picnic or as dangerous and exciting as any thrill-seeker could imagine. Close to shore one may encounter pressure ridges as much as sixty feet high. Beyond these the ice may extend level and unbroken for many miles. But when one begins to approach the open water he finds himself on ice that is different from anything most people have ever experienced. As you walk along you begin to feel swells going under you. You are gently lifted up and set down, again. The ice underfoot has become granular like rock salt. You ram the ice pick attached to your harpoon shaft into the ice and, if solid enough, you take another step forward then repeat the process, jab, step, jab, step. Now the swells are getting higher and coming faster. You feel yourself lifted high above the surrounding ice field then a moment later you are dropped into a deep valley. It is so steep-walled you cannot see out. You walk fast, for to stop an instant would be to sink in the ground-up ice. At a time like this it is nice to be pulling an oogruk sled on which a kayak is resting. Usually the hunting is done from kayaks at the edge of the ice pack but sometimes it is done afoot on narrow leads or at blow holes where the seals and oogruk come up for air.

Hunting twenty-five or thirty miles offshore on the ice is always dangerous business for if the wind should change suddenly and blow offshore, the ice pack may be set adrift before the hunters can get ashore. They run the chance of losing their lives when the ice breaks up mid-channel or if it holds together to wind up on the Siberian shore. There are many tales of hunters who actually did land in Siberia and were able to return to Alaska some years later. None of the hunters was lost during our stay in Shishmaref but several had had narrow escapes, losing some or all of their dogs in the mishaps.

The ice hunters must have a warning five or six hours in advance that the wind is going to change else they would never get in before it parted from the shore. The signal they get comes from Ear Mountain which lies behind the village on the mainland. By watching the cloud formations around this peak the natives know when to come in. We recall seeing many times those little black streaks on the ice, each representing a dogteam, and all converging on the village. Then, only a few moments after the last team had come ashore, the ice would break off and drift to sea.

Late in June the hunters abandoned the dogteam and kayak hunting and resorted to oomiak hunting. By this time the shore ice was gone and the sea was full of large floes on and around which the seals and oogruk and an occasional walrus could be found. Hunting was done mostly by rifle although some of the hunters still preferred to use the harpoon. In the spring most of the oogruk would sink when killed, but these were retrieved with an iron gang hook made for the purpose.

The first oogruk taken each spring was accorded special honors. When brought ashore a little grass would be placed in its mouth or fresh water would be poured in its mouth in order to placate the seal god so it would not be offended and so that it would continue to provide food for the Eskimos.

Along the beach in the shelter of a sand dune, if possible, were the oogruk camps. A typical camp consisted of a tent or two, a heap of driftwood and a number of racks on which oogruk meat was drying. Here and there on the ground stretched oogruk skins were staked to dry and nearby were numbers of sealskin *pokes* already filled with blubber and dried meat. All the labor of butchering the oogruk and seals, skinning, flensing, drying, packing, storing was the work of the women. And practically every operation was accomplished with a single tool, the little semi-lunar knife they called an *oolu*. Not only were the hides stretched and dried, the meat hung on racks and eventually stored in bags and the blubber rendered but other important by-products were processed. For example, the intestines were saved to be inflated and dried, thereafter to be used in making rain parkas and windows. Bladders were processed, also, to be used as containers for oil or water and seal skins were taken off intact to be used as *pokes* in which most Eskimo food was stored for the winter.

In this season the children were as industrious as their parents. The larger boys and girls gathered driftwood not only for present use but to be stacked above the high tide line for winter use. They also roamed the tundra gathering duck and goose eggs and snaring ptarmigan. Children too small for gathering driftwood minded still smaller children for their mothers.

June found Toni and me roaming the beaches and tundra almost as free as the children. There was no night and little if any wind. The sun shone almost continuously and even though it never got above sixty degrees fahrenheit on the seashore we were warm and comfortable since temperatures like everything else are relative and it was now ninety degrees warmer than our winter fare.

Seabirds were now arriving and nesting in the vicinity by the thousands. We gathered gull eggs, found them an excellent substitute for hens' eggs which of course were not procurable. Occasionally we took an egg from the nest of an eider duck or emperor goose but found them a little too rich for our palates when better eggs were available. We preferred above all others the tiny and delicately-flavored eggs of the arctic tern. But any fresh egg, be it from loon, squaw duck or shitepoke was a welcome diversion after a winter's diet of powdered eggs which at best could only substitute for scrambled eggs.

Sometimes on our forays we would run into little bands of children wandering on the pathless tundra, willy nilly, and living off the country. They generally carried ptarmigan snares, bows and blunted arrows, or an old shotgun with a pocketful of hand-loads. Often they were hard to approach, seeming to melt away whenever they saw another human being approaching. Since there was no night, these children would wander until tired or sleepy then lie down for a nap on a dry hummock. I remember coming across a boy, dead to the world, lying on his back with his shotgun by his side, his eyes protected from the sun by wooden snow goggles. A short distance away I had seen a rusty musket lying on the tundra. I went back and got this and laid it beside him. Then I removed his own gun and placed it at some distance behind him. Leaving him, I had not gone far before I came across a bleached human skull. This I carried back and placed it between his knees, facing him. I then took a position behind him some twenty feet away and tossed clods at him until he woke up. He sat up and rubbed his eyes as if partially snow-blind. Then he saw the skull and stared at it motionless, apparently trying to collect his wits. I saw him fumble for his gun without taking his eyes off the skull. When his hand came up with the musket that I had planted, he stared at it a long while then he slowly twisted around until he could see me. I'll never forget the sheepish grin that stole over his face. Without a word he gathered up his shotgun and his game bag and wandered away.

As soon as the beach was free of ice we spent a great deal of time beachcombing. Every day, and particularly after a storm, we would find ivory on the sand. This was usually old ivory, colored fragments of tusks and teeth of both walrus and mammoth. Sometimes we found complete tusks of walrus and the small temporary teeth of mammoth usually dark brown or black in color. Then there were the teeth of pleistocene horses and bison and other ungulates that formerly lived on Seward peninsula as well as all parts of interior Alaska.

Our prize find was collected in an odd way. We were walking the beach when I stepped on what I thought was a small length of driftwood. But as I walked on I recalled that the piece had sprung up when I stepped on it, indicating that it was curved. This suggested a tusk so I returned and picked it up. Sure enough, it was a tusk but not from a walrus as it was too round. It turned out to be a coal black mammoth tusk or at least the tusk of some species of primitive elephant that dwelt in Alaska in remote times. However, it was only about ten inches long and an inch in diameter, not the tip or core of a larger tusk but of fine texture more like the complete tusk of a pigmy elephant. I have never heard of another like it but have always hoped its mate might still turn up.

Only a very few types of sea shells were ever cast up on our beach, all of which were unknown to us. One was obviously a whelk and these were eaten by the Eskimos. But none of the others were alive. Some looked like clamshells, but very thick and heavy, others like periwinkles. None were large or spectacular so we paid little attention to them.

Peculiar rock formations or crystals in clusters were to be found on the beach at times. They looked like stone flowers or sunbursts, no two being alike. We learned later that they were calcite pseudomorphs after glauberite and were quite rare. The few that we took out with us eventually found their way into a museum collection.

The eider ducks and other sea birds returning to the Arctic used the beach as a guide, since at the beginning of their migration both the sea and the tundra were white, frozen wastes, while the beach was bare and black by contrast. They flew so low they could be taken easily by boys and old men using the *bolas*. These bolas consisted of about eight walrus teeth strung on sinew lines about a yard long and joined together at the end in a knot which was sometimes feathered like a shuttlecock. To use the bolas, one holds the walrus teeth weights in the left hand and the feathered knot in his right, the lines being stretched taut between the two hands. When the oncoming ducks have reached the proper distance, the left hand releases the weights and at the same time a cartwheel motion is made by the right which then lets go to send the bolas spread out like a fan in front of the oncoming ducks. If one of these birds is unfortunate enough to touch one of the lines, its walrus tooth weight immediately winds the sinew line around it. That is to be expected. But then the most unexpected thing happens. All the other weights being snubbed by the one that has struck the duck are instantly checked, and with seeming intelligence, turn and assist their comrade in enmeshing the hapless duck with all their lines, rendering it helpless and bearing it to the ground like a ton of lead.

As soon as the snow disappeared from the tundra we began to explore the island north and south of the village. We soon found that our island had long been the home of man as there were signs of long-abandoned igloos and middens the full length of the habitable portion of the island. Out of deference to the present inhabitants we did no digging but felt certain that some-day archaeologists would find here the answers to many of the problems concerning man's antiquity in America for from this very spot one could see the Asiatic mainland on any clear day.

Certain parts of the island had been reserved for burial in the remote past. At that time the bodies were not actually buried but placed in boxes on the surface. Then a tripod of drift logs was placed over the grave on which *killed* property of the deceased was hung. But as time went on there would be years when no driftwood would be deposited upon these shores so the inhabi-tants would retrieve wood from the cemetery, piece by piece. Eventually nothing would be left there except the plank on which the body rested. The cemetery, with the graves placed side by side along the length of a sand dune, took on the appearance of an abandoned railway track, the nails removed and the ties rotting in place. But close examination would reveal ribs and small bones impressed in the rotten wood while in the low places beside the dune corresponding to the borrow pits along a rail-road could be found the bleached long bones and the skulls.

The local Eskimos paid no attention whatever to the human bones lying about. We saw boys playing catch with skulls or using them for targets. Once I used a skull to mark the location of an eider duck's nest from which I intended to purloin an egg or two as they were laid. Then one day I saw an Eskimo doing something there and I wondered if I had offended him by carrying the skull to a hummock and leaving it there. Anyway, after he had left, I returned to the place to see what he had done. Instead of one skull on the hummock there were now three, all facing each other as if they were having a chat.

We were told that one particularly large mass of bones resulted from a massacre that took place in the very distant past. It seems the Shishmaref people were having a dance in the *kazhgie,* a large clubhouse or meeting place, when a war party from Igloo village arrived. Some of the warriors got on top the kazhgie with their spears and others built a fire at the tunnel entrance to prevent escape. Everyone, including women and children, were speared as they tried to leave the burning igloo. That night a hunting party returned to the village and finding their friends and neighbors murdered took after the enemy in order to take revenge. They followed the tracks of the party all the next day, keeping out of sight. When the war party made camp, the avengers waited until all were asleep, then crept in and cut their throats. That is, all except one. This man was so nimble they could not kill him although they struck him repeatedly with their spears. Eventually he escaped and the avenging party returned to Shishmaref.

Some years later the Shishmaref people were invited to a big party at Igloo. During this affair one of the Igloo men made a speech, proposing that Shishmaref and Igloo end their feuding and concentrate on fighting off the Siberians who periodically raided the coast to carry off women. To demonstrate his point he removed his parka, showing his body to be covered with huge scars of battle. He compared his scarred and weakened body to the Eskimo people as a whole, admonishing them to stop warring between themselves before it was too late. The Shishmaref people told us that this was the end of the Eskimo wars. The story was quite a surprise to us as we had never pictured the Eskimos as warriors at any time, not that they would be afraid to fight, but because they were such nice people you couldn't picture them angry or desperate.

After the third week in June, the ice was so broken up we expected a ship momentarily. The sun didn't set now but would dip to the horizon at midnight then immediately rise again. Actually the sun did dip partially beneath the horizon since we were slightly below the arctic circle but to the eye, the complete sun was still visible. Nevertheless, just at that moment, it seemed there was always a slight chill breeze, then it would start to warm up again. But, by habit or instinct, the birds settled down for the brief night even though it was broad daylight and at this time we usually went egg picking on the next island north. About three a.m. we would return and cook our supper. Any natives in the vicinity, seeing our smoke, would come to the house for medicine or just to visit a while. By six a.m. we would dismiss our guests and get to bed, wearing black masks. But sleep would not come for every few minutes we would have to get up and rush to the window to see if there was a ship in sight.

Then one day we heard it. *Tray-may! Umiak-puk!* (It comes! Steamboat!) We rushed out but there was no ship. It was only the mukluk telegraph relaying a message from camp to camp that a ship had been sighted somewhere south of us.

Several days later we saw the sail. It was the four-masted *C. S. Holmes*, Captain John Backlund, Sr., out of Seattle. It had freight for us but it could not get in. One day it would appear two or three miles south of the village. Then it would disappear for a few days. Then we saw it again four or five miles offshore and north of the village.

In the meanwhile the little tug *Kobuk* sneaked in from Nome on July 7th, the first boat of the season. Aboard were Mr. and Mrs. Sam Magids, traders of Deering, who stayed with us long enough for Bess Magids to teach Toni how to bake bread. On the ninth the *Holmes* finally made it in and discharged her cargo of coal and groceries. The same day the mailboat *Silverwave*, Capt. John Hegness, called in to pick up freight it had cached near here last fall when it was unable to make it in to Kotzebue.

It never rains but it pours. Nine months without a ship and then three on the same day. The third was the *Hazel*, belonging to the Biological Survey. In charge was L. J. Palmer of the Biological Survey, Carl Lomen of Nome, D. M. Le Bourdais, noted writer, and several others. Palmer was doing reindeer research and expressed a desire to visit our herds. So we acquired a skinboat with sail and started off to visit the Serpentine river herd which was pastured near Cape Krusenstern, about ten miles from the village.

Everything went well for a while as we sailed across Shishmaref Inlet but a strong wind came up suddenly and put us on the beach. We were not too far from the herd so we decided to walk. I was in advance carrying my shotgun. Since we had no food with us and very likely were stuck for the night I was thinking of provisions. Presently a ptarmigan got up and I knocked it down. I heard a few muffled comments behind me but thought nothing of it. Just then another ptarmigan rose and I potted it, also. By then I was aware the men behind me were discussing the legality of my hunting. Up until that moment it had never occurred to me that hunting laws existed in Alaska.

By the time I had enough ptarmigan to go around the white men had decided that, because of the emergency, I was justified in shooting the birds and nobody held back when they were served up that evening.

The trip to the herds was a treat at that time of year. It was too early for mosquitos to be a problem as their season is roughly from July 15th to the middle of August. But the wildflowers were in full bloom and we saw many species, some of which were not present on our island. These included primroses, marsh marigolds, poppies and various heather blossoms. We saw monkshood, fireweed, blue gentians and fernweed, sometimes called lousewort. Besides, there were those world-spanning cosmopolitans, the buttercups and dandelions, and some flowers we couldn't name.

As I had feared, the wind made it impossible for us to return to Shishmaref on schedule but nobody thought of sleeping in broad daylight so we just explored throughout the sunny night. We finally got off and returned to the village about eight a.m. the next morning, whereupon the *Hazel* lifted anchor and continued her trip northward.

We had heard the U.S. Revenue Cutter *Bear* was in the vicinity and had expected a call from Captain C. S. Cochran. Several times we had seen her smoke but she was far out to sea. Then one day we saw her heading south. Sometime later the word came to us that the *Bear* had never gotten beyond Cape Blossom, near Kotzebue. The ice was particularly bad that season and in battling it she had damaged her propeller so bad it was necessary to pass up the Barrow trip that season and return to Seattle for repairs.

*   *   *   *

A DUCK DRIVE

About the middle of July each year the pintail ducks moult their flight feathers and for a week or so are unable to fly. Anticipating this handicap the male birds leave the females that are busy with their broods and fly inland to a region dotted with small lakes and ponds. There they settle down to grow new feathers and to get rolling fat in this period of relative inactivity. The Eskimos know about this and each year stage a somewhat ceremonial duck hunt. Probably I shouldn't say *ceremonial* since there was no ceremony as such. But in this particular annual hunt no firearms were allowed and the hunt was conducted exactly as it was in more primitive times before the advent of white men and their murderous weapons. I count myself lucky to have been invited on this outing as I doubt that many, if any, other whites ever had participated.

The party which included every able-bodied Eskimo in the vicinity assembled at the mouth of the Serpentine river on the 14th of July. When we took off we must have made a strange procession. Ahead were half a dozen kayaks side by side and equally spaced from bank to bank. Behind them came a string of oomiaks single file and midstream. Each oomiak was loaded with women and children, a few dogs and vast quantities of gear and camping material.

The men in the kayaks were armed with duck darts which are hurled by means of a throwing device known in other parts of the world as the *atlatl*. These darts had long ivory points, barbed on both edges the entire length. Below the point and set into the wooden shaft were three barbed branches. In use, if one should miss with the point, there was still the chance that the branches would catch the bird by the neck or around a leg or wing. I saw many near-misses pay off because of these ingenious appendages. The kayak hunters were deadly accurate with their darts up to, say sixty feet or so. Any duck found swimming on the river ahead of the kayaks sooner or later wound up in the soup.

As we proceeded up the winding river, no one spoke a word and the paddles were dipped noiselessly so as not to frighten the ducks in the numberless ox bow lakes beside the river which testified to the many former courses the river had taken across this flat land. Whenever we reached a promising lake the kayak men would land and, taking their kayaks on their shoulders, would walk silently toward the lake and their expected quarry. As soon as the ducks would see the hunters they would swim rapidly to the very center of the lake. Then the hunters would launch their kayaks and move towards the closely-packed flock. This would be the signal for the ducks to start swimming en masse towards the shore opposite the oncoming kayaks.

In the meanwhile the oomiaks had landed and the occupants had started crawling through the grass to be in a position to intercept the ducks as soon as they reached the shore. The poor pintails didn't have a chance. Darts got the laggards and the moment the main flock started climbing up the bank to hide in the grass they were met by a horde of men, women and children. At first they simply grabbed a duck in each hand, wrung their necks, dropped them, grabbed another brace and repeated the process. Those ducks that did reach cover had no better luck. As they lay flattened out in the grass with necks outstretched they were perfect targets for the women and boys armed with clubs. Even those that were perfectly camouflaged had no chance either since little girls with dogs on leashes soon sought them out.

After each drive was completed, the ducks were sacked up and carried to the oomiaks whereupon we would all take off for the next lake. When evening came all of the oomiaks were emptied of contents, hauled out on the riverbank and turned up on edge where, propped up by paddles, they served as shelters. Now the pots and the oilcans were dug out of the heap and preparations were made for a banquet. While some gathered willow branches for fuel others went off for drinking water or to search for eggs. Anyone not otherwise occupied sat down and plucked ducks.

When an Eskimo plucks a duck he is not too particular about the job, especially at this time of year when the birds are full of pinfeathers. In fact, they seemed to relish pinfeathers, chewing up the soft parts and spitting out the rest. When they dressed a duck all the edible entrails were left attached to the bird by their natural connections. The birds, head, feet and all, were tossed into an oil can to be boiled with about half a teaspoonful of salt to the five gallon can.

The number of ducks a healthy, hungry Eskimo can eat at a sitting is appalling. About the only limiting factor is the supply. From what I could see, six ducks would be a conservative average meal for one person, topped off with a dozen or so semi-incubated eggs and numberless cups of water or tea. When an Eskimo eats a duck there is nothing left that would interest a hungry fox. He eats it inside, outside, head, feet and all. I saw them open the beaks to get at the tongue, and gnaw off the short feathers from the top of the head. The boiled eggs, although already incubating, presented no problem. They would first eat what remained of the yolk, play with the embryo chick for a time, stretching out its back, legs and wings, and then, down the hatch. I was never offered an egg with a chick in it, but if it was merely addled and not incubated, that was for me, with accompanying smiles and hospitable gestures.

We raided the lakes adjacent to the river for three days and then returned to the village bearing fourteen gunnysacks of ducks for home use and for those who couldn't go. I suppose there are people who would bitterly condemn the Eskimos for raiding the ducks when they were helpless. However, they did it only once a year and left no crippled birds to die unnoticed of lead poisoning. I doubt that their hunt had any more depleting effect on the duck population than a Sunday's shoot on a marsh near any big city in the states during the migration. In any event, they did it for two thousand years before we got here with our firearms.

The day I got back from the duck drive Toni and I got a chance to go to Nome on the mailboat, *Silverwave*. It was only deck passage which we shared with a dozen others but it was better than nothing, besides we had a lot of business to attend to in Nome. Aft the pilot house there was considerable deck space. A large tarpaulin had been stretched tent-like across the boom, making a large shelter. Beneath this we laid our sleeping bags in a close row beside the others.

We carried aboard all the nice, fat ducks I had brought home from the drive and turned them over to Kobuk Red, the cook. We had envisioned roast duck but that was not to be. Kobuk had a mad on and was quitting as soon as they reached port. Poor fellow, we couldn't blame him. He must have stood nearly seven feet tall when he could straighten out, but the galley ceiling was barely six and hardly wide enough to accommodate the stove. Besides, with the deck passengers, he had about two dozen to cook for. But he didn't throw the ducks overboard. Instead, he took a cleaver and hacked them into two-inch chunks. These he dumped into a large pot and added whatever vegetables he had on hand. The result was a huge duck stew and not at all bad. That ended Kobuk's cooking. He took to his berth and didn't leave it until we reached Nome two days later. The passengers, all sourdoughs, thereupon took over the galley and cooked for themselves in relays.

Enroute to Nome we got ashore at Wales, Teller Mission, and at Teller where we met old friends and made new ones that have lasted a lifetime. Among them were Reverend Dahle and family at the mission, and Mrs. Billy Marx, Miss Vollmer and Mr. and Mrs. Tom Peterson at Teller. Tom is gone but the rest were still in Teller after more than thirty years.

We spent the next two weeks in Nome enjoying white man's civilization or as much of it as they had there, and shopping, both for ourselves and the natives. For even though Nome itself was an outpost it had many attractions that Shishmaref and all points north of Nome lacked. For instance, it had a movie and a newspaper and a hotel where one could enjoy a bathtub bath. There was a bakery and a restaurant, too, where people gathered in the evenings. And speaking of the bakery, it was the North Pole bakery that offered us a cat and promised to have it ready for us when we sailed. We had been looking for a cat for two reasons. First, because none of the children in Shishmaref had ever seen a cat, and second because we were troubled somewhat with mice. Not the ordinary house mice but fat, wild fur-bearing mice that lived in the grass on the dunes but would come in the house whenever they had the chance.

The Nome people were most hospitable and before a week had passed we had met nearly everyone in town. I recall meeting Tony Polet and his family; the Mike Walsh's, the Maynards who had the newspaper, the Lomens who were in everything. Then there was Frank Martin, Dan Crowley, Lawrence Kerr, Father La Fortune, and Bishop Peter Trimble Rowe. Tony Polet ran a store catering to tourists and specializing in carved ivory and fur. Walsh was a pioneer mining man and the Maynards' newspaper, the *Nome Nugget,* is still going strong after more than fifty years. The senior Lomen was the district judge and the boys were variously engaged in the reindeer business, the lighterage business, ran a couple mailboats, and operated a drug store. Real pioneers, they were the kind of people you'd be proud to know. Frank Martin was a fur buyer and Dan Crowley was a reindeer man, employed by the Lomens. Father La Fortune was the King Island sky pilot who brought his Eskimo charges to Nome each summer so they could earn dollars carving ivory for the tourists and then wintering with them on the island. Bishop Rowe was famous for his far-flung Episcopal diocese, stretching from Ketchikan to Point Hope, the largest in the world.

We were taken out to the third beach line, a prehistoric shoreline, where huge gold dredges were operating on the pay streak some eighty feet beneath the surface. This operation was in permafrost (a word that hadn't been coined then) so it was necessary to thaw the ground ahead of the dredge. This was accomplished by a maze of pipes through which water was pumped. The *B. Desperate Hyde,* the huge Yuba dredge that we

had seen last year, looked like a battleship nearly out of its ele-
ment. It floated in a pond of its own creation, digging away at
the bank in front of it and repiling the gravel behind after it had
been washed for its gold. In this manner it carried its little lake
wherever it went and from the size and extent of the tailings piles
it had gone a long way.

One afternoon we strolled down to the Sand Spit where the
King Island Eskimos habitually set up their camp and spent the
summer carving ivory cribbage boards, billikins, paper knives,
etc. for sale to the tourists. It was a typical Eskimo camp, the
shelters being oomiaks propped up on edge by paddles in the
protection of which the men carved ivory and the women sewed,
cooked, and minded their numerous children. It was while in the
process of taking a picture of the scene that I saw, in the ground
glass viewer, a wild-eyed Eskimo coming at me with a butcher
knife. I had barely time to deflect him with my heavy camera
case when two other Eskimos caught the fellow and disarmed
him. He struggled and trembled, apparently from great fright,
when they led him away. Presently the men came back and apolo-
gized for the young man's behavior. They referred to him as a
wild boy who had never been off King Island before and apparently thought my camera could hex him or something. Anyway
he was the first and only Eskimo I ever saw who didn't want his
picture taken. It may be different now but in those days I made
it a practice always to give the Eskimos prints of any picture I
took of them. The happy result was that on almost any fine day
an entire family in all its finery might appear requesting that I
take its picture.

On the third of August, the *Boxer* arrived at Nome from the
south, providing us with an opportunity to get back to our station. We began rounding up our purchases and getting them
aboard; things for ourselves, for the natives and for the station.
We had particularly made the trip to have branding irons made
for the reindeer which were going into an organized herd or reindeer company that fall. Then there was the cat. Just before sailing
time the cat was delivered. It was tied up securely in the depths
of a flour gunny and we were expressly cautioned to keep her
there until we got her aboard the *Boxer* and well out to sea. We
should have smelled a rat. We did take one little peep to allay our
sub-conscious misgivings, but the glimpse pleased us no end.
What we saw was apparently a beautiful blue maltese tabby.

Aboard ship and under sail we immediately liberated our

feline. We were in for a shock. What bounded, spitting and snarling, out of the sack was nothing but a black alley cat liberally dusted with flour which gave it a bluish cast. Its ears had been frozen down to nubbins and its tail had been broken in at least three places, making definite angles at each break. Several other areas of the body were scarred and furless, evidence of frequent brushes with local malemutes or winter's blizzards. We had acquired a typical *pig in a poke* but since we were out nothing we could laugh off the joke. At any rate it would be the finest cat in Shishmaref.

Aboard the *Boxer* was a mail pouch full of first class mail for us. But because it was a locked pouch that couldn't be opened until we reached Wales we had to wait again for letters, many of which were already a year old. Eventually, however, we reached Wales and got at our mail. That night as we sailed north between the Diomede Islands the sea was like oil and the northern sky was blood red. But we were all but oblivious to the magnificent scenery. We were sitting on deck reading our first mail from home in a year, ninety-eight letters from a world that seemed already like a distant planet.

Chapter XI

THE CO-OPERATIVES

When Toni and I first contracted to go to Shishmaref we were advised that our job would encompass a great deal more than mere teaching. There would be medical duties and social welfare. By courtesy we would also keep the weather records, make bird counts, collect certain vermin from the flipper pits of walrus, etc., I believe between us we had some fourteen different duties to perform for some branch of the Federal Government, mostly by courtesy. But two most important assignments from our own office we did have. They were, first, to organize the various private reindeer herds into a Reindeer Co-operative Herd and second, to organize a Co-operative Store. These were musts.

On this trip of the *Boxer* was the first stock for the co-operative store as well as lumber to build the store building. So, immediately upon arrival at Shishmaref we stored the Co-op goods in the school buildings and unloaded the lumber on a lot just east of the teacher's cottage. We started construction at once with plans I had drawn on a short board. I no longer remember the dimensions but they were adequate. At the rear we built a lean-to appendage for the quarters of the storekeeper and his family. This we faced with turf for insulation against the cold like any igloo in the village.

At first we had a terrible time convincing the stockholders that they still had to pay for their groceries even though they owned stock. What made this doubly hard to put across was the fact that heretofore on several occasions they had pooled their resources for a cargo of winter supplies. And when they arrived each family took its share and went home with it without paying anything. Now, they found, they had invested their money in stock but got no groceries. How come? What kind of a racket was this, anyway? But, little by little, the good and sensible villagers came to understand that part of their investment was represented by the building and the rest by goods on the shelves which would earn money for them as the stock was turned over. And besides, from now on there would always be a good supply of groceries, hardware and dry goods on hand at reasonable prices.

I only hope it worked out that way. Previously they had been robbed by local traders both on the price paid for fur and the prices charged for supplies. Under the co-operative, the trappers could turn their furs in to their own store for credit and then when the furs were sold on the Seattle Fur Exchange, receive the exact credit the furs had brought. With an honest and intelligent store management they couldn't lose.

The reindeer deal was more involved. Back in the 1890's, Dr. Sheldon Jackson had talked the Federal Government into setting the Eskimo up in the reindeer business with deer imported from Siberia, and with Lapp herders from Norway to show them how. The Eskimos co-operated, although their heart really wasn't in it, and the deer thrived and multiplied. In almost no time nearly every mature male Eskimo had a herd of reindeer and a piece of tundra assigned to him for range. They had gotten their deer by serving as apprentice herders who collected no wages but at the end of their apprenticeship could drive home a small herd of reindeer which rapidly multiplied as there were rules against killing does, which had one or two fawns annually, and most of the natives preferred seal meat, anyhow.

Now the range was getting scarce or over-grazed. Besides, it was becoming increasingly difficult to get apprentices to work for nothing except a passel of deer that brought no profit, anyway. The trouble at Shishmaref, aside from the natural reluctance of the natives to leave the seashore, was the fact that these little herds were scattered over some 3000 square miles of range and nobody was raising enough steers to drive to market, providing there was a market, which there was not. So my job was to talk the deer owners into organizing a co-operative, get the deer into one big herd, and employ paid herders. Then, at an appointed time and place, they could butcher the marketable steers, load them on the *Boxer* or a cold storage barge and eventually market them in the states.

It had taken me all winter at innumerable reindeer meetings to effect the organization on paper. The trip to Nome to have branding irons made was the next step. Now we were ready to take the third — to build a corral and count the herd so that shares could be apportioned, accordingly. On August 27th I crossed Shishmaref Inlet to the mainland near the mouth of the Arctic river where the corral was being built, to assist in the count. The corral was a huge affair built to accommodate 5000 deer without crowding, complete with chute and holding pens. It was constructed of driftwood, coal sacks and wire. I had pro-

vided the coal sacks, but unbelievably, the wire was provided by
the Western Union Telegraph Co. although they didn't know it.
It was part of the loot abandoned in Teller in 1866 when the
telegraph line being constructed overland across Canada, Alaska
and Siberia to Europe was abandoned upon the successful laying
of the Atlantic Cable. At long last the wire had been put to good
use.

We ran the entire herd of approximately 5000 reindeer
through in two long days. The ownership of each deer was determined by its earmarks and then given the company brand. At
first we tried to brand on the hip but immediately gave that up
as the hair was too thick to reach the hide. Thereafter we branded
on the cheek where the hair is short. Since a herd always mills
the same way we would put the brand on the side always on the
outside of the herd. Thus a deer from a herd that milled clock-
wise would be branded on the left cheek, or if counter-clockwise,
on the right side. While the count went on male calves were
castrated and steers ready for market were shunted into holding
pens. The rest were turned out immediately.

Even though the work was hard, there was also plenty fun.
After a shift I could always take the shotgun and go off to shoot
ptarmigan. Brant, too, were very plentiful as were the little brown
cranes that everybody called *sandhills*. I saw a peculiar thing
that fall when the birds were collecting preparatory to flying south.
First, a single crane took off, calling loudly, and flew as near
straight up as it could. After it had reached an elevation of several
hundred feet it leveled off, still calling, and inscribed a large
circle over the tundra, perhaps taking in a thousand acres. Presently another crane rose to follow it, and then another and
another, all calling like the leader. Then I noticed the leader was
shortening the diameter of his circle and more cranes went up
to join the aerial procession. Eventually all the cranes within
hearing must have been gathered up in this manner, whereupon
the flock headed south and we saw no more of them that season.

The brant were getting ready to go, too. We noticed them
everyday practicing all sorts of maneuvers no doubt designed to
test and strengthen the wings of the young birds. Eventually the
leaders were satisfied that all could make the trip and off they
went to more salubrious winter climates. They must have been
the avian bell-wethers for very shortly all the other waterfowl
species in the district took off in the same direction.

There were a few small mammals around, too. We saw

several red foxes hanging around and on several well-drained knobs there were ground squirrels which the Eskimos called *sik sik*. These were trapped for their hides which made good summer parkas or linings for winter clothes. Then there were mice and shrews. The mice were seed eaters like the squirrels but I often wondered what the shrews ate unless it was the mice. I recall one night the Eskimo who shared my tent, awoke and slapped his ear a terrific whack. Then he picked up a tiny dead shrew by the tail, examined it quizzically, saying, "This fellow try to eat it me!" Little did he know the truth of his assertion for we are told this bloodthirsty little carnivore must eat its weight in flesh and blood every six hours or die.

Later that fall the *Boxer* called in southbound and took off a load of reindeer meat for the Seattle market. Apparently the co-operative was off to a good start. But as we left the country the following spring we were unable to keep in touch with it or any other reindeer activity in Alaska. We did learn, however, that the industry had fallen on evil days and had almost completely collapsed for various assigned reasons. Some said abandoning of our close-herding methods resulted in the deer getting wild or lost and in some known instances joining the caribou herds and going off with them. Others said wolves descended on the herds and wiped them out. Still others said the deer had become so numerous they had destroyed their range and had died of starvation. The truth no doubt lies somewhere between these reasons or might be a combination of the three. Besides some philosopher might question the wisdom of attempting to change a marine hunting people to a tundra herding people overnight. But on Nunivak island and at several other localities there are still reindeer herds maintained with profit and giving promise that the reindeer business may yet become important in the economy of the far north.

Chapter XII

A VILLAIN AND
AN ESKIMO PHILOSOPHER

While I was absent from the village, several things of importance had occurred there. First, the *Teddy Bear* had gone by without landing but aboard was Knud Rasmussen, the famous Danish anthropologist who, on the Fifth Thule Expedition, had just completed a trip from Greenland, across Arctic Canada and around northern Alaska. How I wanted to meet him. We learned later that he crossed to East Cape, Siberia, where he was allowed only thirty minutes ashore. But we found that everywhere he went he was able to make himself understood speaking the Greenland Eskimo tongue and in the half hour in Siberia he had found the information he was seeking.

The other incident of importance was the arrival of the *Nome* of Nome with a trader and his outfit aboard, moving in on us. This trader had conceived the idea of crossing arctic white foxes with blue foxes to achieve a platinum shade that apparently had great possibilities with the trade. For several years he had had a confederate settled on the northern end of the island, feeding several pens of white foxes while he rustled capital in the East. Now at long last he had arrived with knocked-down buildings, pens and trading stock, besides several dozen blue foxes.

Without so much as "by your leave" he began erecting his buildings practically in the local cemetery at one end, and just above the village water ponds at the other. As far as he was concerned Eskimos were not people, but just something to be pushed around and exploited. In this he was not entirely unique as that was quite the common practice of commercial people in that area in those days. For those who voiced mild protests, he had ready promises which immediately satisfied these trusting souls.

At first most of the villagers were enthusiastic about the venture as it created excitement and the prospect of wages to be earned erecting the buildings and pens. There was also the prospect of selling fox feed which could be profitable. And to allay their worst fears he promised to build a nice new fence around the cemetery and to avoid contaminating the water supply.

All the work erecting the buildings and pens was done by

local labor but the wages were never paid in cash. Instead, the workmen had to accept goods from the fox farmer's trading stock at jacked-up prices. And such goods! Again with no respect for Eskimo preference or needs he had brought in such unsalable items as airtight heaters, cheap, gaudy calicos that might have sold in Siberia, and unionsuits. It might have been excusable for a rank outsider to have brought in such ridiculous trade goods but this man had been in the country long enough to know better. Igloos are never heated; wood is too scarce and precious to be squandered that way. It is to be burned only for cooking. As for the women's cloth overparkas, only ginghams in the softest pastel pinks and blues were acceptable. Green, never! And *unionsuits!* One would have to be insane to put on such a garment. Supposing you were out in 30 below zero weather and you broke through the ice and got your feet wet. How would you get your unionsuit off and dry clothes on before you would freeze to death? Eskimos think of those things.

But that was only the beginning. The ponds were soon contaminated with fox dung and offal; the cemetery fence was never built and the graves were desecrated. He tried to corner the village supply of seal meat used for dog feed so he could import Kotzebue salmon and force the natives to buy his dried fish at twice the price he intended to pay for the seal meat. But thanks to the Eskimos' innate good sense they saw through the plan and also his scheme for getting control of their herds. At first we had feared that his initial plan to reduce the entire village to peonage would succeed. But as we came to know the Eskimo better our fears were put to rest. We knew then that the Eskimos would be there long after the fox farmers had folded up, for they had learned to wrest their living from the land unaided and the fox men were at best parasites who could not survive there without willing hosts.

In the years that followed we often wondered if we had done the right thing by allowing this person to come in without benefit of law or courtesy. We could have, vigilante fashion, harried him from the island. But at best that course could only have postponed the inevitable. The Eskimos had been living in a vacuum. The question being pondered then as it still is in some quarters, was whether or not the vacuum could or should be maintained. There were those who, posing as the Eskimos' friend and protector, favored reservations where the natives could go on living primitive picturesque lives in a vacuum sustained by law. There were others, probably more genuine friends, who considered reservations nothing more than concentration camps or human zoos. These people believed that Eskimos, given a decent break, could live in a white man's world and compete on even terms.

In those days the question was more or less academic. But things were happening. The radio and the aeroplane were beginning to shrink the world and although Shishmaref had seen neither, that was the year that Carl Ben Eielson, the father of Alaskan aviation, landed in Fairbanks. So it was no longer a question of "should the vacuum be maintained" but could it? We felt that it couldn't and shouldn't, and that our job was actually to help prepare the Eskimo for assimilation. So it was not all to the bad that their first contact with white men was not altogether pleasant. It would make them wary and watchful and perhaps the transition of their economy and culture would be made easier by taking it in easy steps and stages.

And what of the villain? I saw him when he left the country. After a long life of trouble-making and frustration he finally withdrew, licked completely by a wornout philosophy.

* * * *

An Eskimo Philosopher

The only gasboat hull in Shishmaref belonged to a progressive Eskimo named William Allockeok. He had acquired the craft from a defunct mining company that owed him money and I had ordered the *Frisco Standard* motor for him the year before. I'll never forget the trouble Allockeok had installing that motor. There was no one to help him and he had no experience with gas engines. Besides, the instruction book that should have accompanied the motor, never arrived. Everything went along all right until it came to the electrical wiring. There was a control box and seeming dozens of wires of different colors issuing from it that had to be attached to something, somewhere. Allockeok tried every combination he could think of but could get no spark. Finally, at his wits end, he went home and got his sleeping bag. Then he made his bed in the boat beside the motor. As he rested, and dreamed and slept, Allockeok tried to conjure up the theory of internal combustion engines and their ignition. And then, after hours of contemplation, miracle or not, he had it! He got up, attached the wires, turned the wheel over, and away she went. He was never troubled by that motor again.

On the 19th of September, Toni and I were invited by Allock-eok to accompany him and his family on a little vacation trip up the Serpentine river before it was time to start school again. We jumped at the chance, for the mosquito season had passed and the fall hunting was on. Besides, I doubt that any other place in the country had such a concentration of waterfowl as the Serpentine river valley.

The stream was well named for like any other river passing through almost level tundra country it wound like a snake, here and there cutting itself off and producing hundreds of ox-bow lakes and ring lakes to left and right. Up this river we chugged all day and when we came to anchor at night we could still see the Eskimo cold-storage mounds at the mouth of the river. We had gone less than five miles airline. We set up a couple of tents on the river bank and in no time were established in what we expected to be our home for a week.

Next morning Allockeok and I took off with our shotguns while the women and children set out to gather cranberries. But first we set our gill nets in the river so they could work in our absence. I had learned from the Eskimos always to carry a gill net in my hip pocket. These were made from heavy Barbour's linen thread such as one would use in sewing leather. Rods and reels are fine for sport but when it is a question of catching fish or starving, use a gill net. It is much more effective and works day and night. When we came back that evening, our nets contained a sampling of grayling, whitefish and ling. Besides, there was a drowned merganzer duck that wasn't able to free itself from the tiny threads.

Shooting was good that day and the next. We bagged many pintails, widgeons, black brant, emperor geese, and ptarmigan. Allockeok even bagged four whistling swans, something I would not have shot myself for sentimental reasons if nothing more, but to an Eskimo, a swan is just so much meat.

The third day was different. One of those sudden northerlies came up so furiously that our tents were blown away and our duffle scattered in all directions. We were forced to take refuge below decks in Allockeok's little gasboat and there we huddled with scarcely room to move. Outside the wind was howling and snow was driving past, horizontally. We had plenty of food, but drinking water was our problem, for the violent gale had stirred up the bottom of the river and the ponds until the water was yellow with the consistency of thin chowder. Over night, winter

had arrived. Nine inches of snow had fallen and every game bird
had been blown out of the country. But that was not all. The
river suddenly ran dry. Fortunately our boat was lashed to the
bank and couldn't topple. But it did look crazy up there when
viewed from the bottom of the river bed. What had happened to
our river I'll never know but I suspect it was something like this.
Bering Strait can act as a bottle neck under certain conditions.
In this instance the northerly gale had blown so continuously
and with such force that the level of the Chukchi sea was lowered
somewhat. The Serpentine, being a tidal river well past our
anchorage, was thereby drained and colder weather had stopped
the flow from the interior. Then when the wind did subside, the
bottle neck at the straits prevented the water from entering our
river for a time. At any event, seven days elapsed before enough
water came back in the river to float our boat.

In the meanwhile we had a glorious opportunity to get
acquainted with Allockeok, his wife and their three small children. Allockeok was a philosopher and a most unusual Eskimo
for these times. As a small boy he had been fostered by a gold
miner and apparently well indoctrinated with white man's ways.
He had never spent a day in school but had taught himself to
write his name and even figure a little. He owned about a thousand reindeer and operated a small store. Besides, he was the
first Shishmaref native to live above ground and was the first
gasboat owner. He was also a successful hunter and trapper. In
fact, nobody in the village could surpass him in anything that
he considered important. But for all that he possessed, for all of
his skill and prowess, Allockeok was not a happy man and that
in itself was unusual in an Eskimo. The reason was that Allockeok
was not a popular man. In the old *nation* as the Eskimos refer to
the bygone days, the best hunter and the richest man would be
the most popular man. For if there was a starving time, they
could always look to the rich man's well-stocked cache for relief.
In those days, when times were rough, people shared everything
down to the last herring. And up until this time the same practice was continued by most of the people. But not Allockeok. If
they would ask for something from his well-stocked shelves
Allockeok would try to explain that the goods there were for sale
and that he expected to be paid for them and to make a small
profit on each item and that this was called *business*. But the old
people knew nothing and cared less about business. What they
did know was that a good man would have shared with them.

Then there was the matter about religion. Most Eskimos had accepted white man's religion without question. But not Allockeok. One night as we huddled in darkness in the hull of his stranded boat, Allockeok gave us a thumbnail sketch of what he had gathered was our religion and what was wrong with it. I was so impressed that I put it down on paper a few days later, almost verbatim.

"White man's *dreligion,* I hear about it," he began. "Bible say long, long ago God he make world. Six days he finish. Gee whiz! Pretty fast work God! Pretty soon He make man. He name, Adam. Adam plenty sorry he got no wife. God see that, so he say, 'All right, Adam. I make 'em wife you fellows.' Adam sleep, God take rib, make Eve. Gee whiz! Funny! Make man mud, women all same bone. No 'stan that me. Adam wake up, see Eve. He like it. Plenty happy now. He marry it.

"God show first people all kinds trees. 'All kinds fruit eat; only apples *never touch it,'* God say.

"Devil, he plenty jealous God. Him like to be boss, too. Pretty soon he make himself snake, all same big worm. Snake tell it Eve, 'Go ahead, eat it! Apples *fine* taste!' Eve, she think about it. Maybe he speak right. She try. Gee whiz! plenty fine taste! Eve give to Adam, he try, too. Him like it.

"Pretty soon Adam and Eve plenty sorry. He remembered it God said, 'Nothing doing, apples!' Plenty sorry Adam and Eve. Plenty red face.

"God hear about that, him plenty mad. He chase it out of garden Adam and Eve. Can't feed it anymore bad people. Adam go to work now hunting, fishing. Eve she make clothes, raise children, plenty cook.

"God all a time plenty mad. He tell it Adam and Eve, 'You listened to me, you happy all time. Never die, children never die. Now, you listen to Devil. All right, you die some day. All your children die sometime. Everybody die some time. Plenty hard work, plenty sick, plenty trouble.

"Well, missionary say we all children of Adam and Eve because they first people. God still curse people because their father and mother long time ago bad. Gee, plenty tough, God. Man make mistake, not right punish him children. I kill it somebody, not right punish my boy. I know *that!*

"God see plenty trouble on earth, he plenty sorry, too. He think about it, 'I make one big mistake! I better try to save now.' Maybe God change mind that time. Look like it.

"Well, Bible say He send His son try to save all people. That boy Jesus Christ. Jesus tell it everybody, 'I'm son of God. You listen to me. I tell it you what to do. You do I tell you to, you go to heaven all right.'

"Some people think about it, that's right. Some people never like Jesus. I think jealous. Pretty soon jealous people kill it Jesus. Gee, too bad! Him good man. He try teach all people right way. After dead, people plenty sorry. People believe it now, he son of God because he try to make people good. That's fine.

"Now people preach about Christ. I travel around Nome, Deering, Candle, Kotzebue, Wales, Teller. I hear it all kinds preachers. Every kind preach little bit different. All preachers say other churches little bit wrong. Gee! Too bad I got no readin'. I like to read Bible myself. I think about it, somebody make plenty mistake. I like to read which one right. I find right kind, I go to church, all right.

"Now people in Shishmaref plenty go to church. Plenty pray because he hear about it, any kind you want, you pray, him come, all right. I think that mistake. All church people plenty poor; igloo empty, bad looks clothes, children all time no grub. All time pray, whatsamatter, never get?

"People think about it, Allockeok him pretty tough man. Never go to church. Rich man, him no good 'tall. Some kind missionary, same way talk. Well, I say no! Allockeok him good man. I never go church because I can't like it all time long face, all-a-time pray. I work hard, plenty save because I got plenty children. Maybe some day I die. Gee whiz! empty house, plenty sorry my family. I never yet see God help hungry Eskimo. I think about it, better help self. Maybe God too busy.

"I heard Bible stories. Long time ago young man he ask Jesus, 'I like to go to heaven. What I'm do now?' Jesus ask, 'You got plenty all kinds stuff?' Young man say, 'Yes.' Jesus say, 'All right, you give every kind to poor people. Then you go to heaven all right.' Young man think hard. Pretty soon red face. Him think about it, 'I'm work hard, plenty save. Other people no work, no save. All time lazy. I think not right divide up with same kind of people.' That young man go to hell. Well, I'm same kind man. I like same kind people. Same kind people in hell, I like it, too. Preacher say hell plenty hot. All right! I like it change. Alaska all-a-time plenty cold. Maybe hell fine for Eskimo!"

Chapter XIII

THE FALL FISHERY—
DISASTER IN THE HERDS

A few days after we got home there was a general exodus to the river where we had recently been stranded as the annual tomcod run was about due. Over night a tent city sprang up at the mouth of the Serpentine which the natives called *Abnoruk*. After the families were settled, nets and seines were brought out of caches to be repaired and otherwise gotten in readiness. For several days gill nets were set out and a quantity of whitefish and grayling were taken. These were eaten fresh as there were hardly more than enough for present purposes. Then came the tomcod! They were seined in such numbers that a single seine load would fill an oomiak. Women and children armed with large wooden platters scooped up the wriggling fish and dumped them into tubs by which they were divided equally among the families participating in the fishery. Later, these tomcod were strung on lines and hung on racks to be dried for winter use.

Shortly after completion of the tomcod run, the herring arrived. One could easily trace the course of the oncoming schools across the lagoon by the cloud of shrieking, diving gulls following them overhead. As they came nearer we could see the water churn and boil by the untold thousands of fish immediately beneath the surface.

These were the most unusual herring, at least a foot in length, firm, fat, and iridescent. It seemed a shame that they were destined to be dogfeed but the run came too late to make up a pack and get it out the same season. They were too oily to dry and there was no wood for smoking. None were salted either since Eskimos do not care for salt fish. A few were frozen for human consumption during the winter when they are eaten raw and frozen as a delicacy known as *ko-ak*.

By far the greater part of the catch was buried in shallow pits beside the river where it froze almost immediately. At intervals throughout the winter the men would go to Abnoruk whenever they needed a supply of dogfeed or bait for their fox traps whereupon they would be chopped out of the pits with axes.

As soon as the tomcod and herring fishery ended the natives

beat a hasty retreat to the village since any day now the lagoon would freeze and they wanted to get their outfits home by oomiak if possible. And it was the completion of this fishery that determined the date for the opening of school for until it was over and the fishermen got home there would be no children whether the bell rang or not.

On the sixth of October we opened school with only twenty-nine students answering the call. However, more families were arriving daily and before the week was out practically all of our prospective students were enrolled.

That week we realized for the first time how really futile our efforts at educating these youngsters had been. In four months virtually everything we had taught out of books was seemingly forgotten. Not a word of English had been uttered, heard nor read by any of these children in all that time. Very likely not a bath had been taken, nor clothes changed, nor hair cut or combed, nor even a face washed in the same period. Our efforts seemed hopeless, useless. And yet, in a few days they were again speaking English, singing the school songs, writing beautifully, reading audibly. When their hair was again washed and trimmed and combed back with generous applications of vaseline the boys lost their wild appearance. Before long they had lost their timid wild animal behavior and we were acquainted again. Perhaps, after all, we hadn't lost ground. But there was a question whether we had gained any, either.

*   *   *   *

On the twenty-third of October the village was alerted by a lone dogteam dashing across the ice of the inlet toward the village, from the direction of Arctic River. Everyone knew instinctively that something was wrong in the reindeer herds and waited silently to hear the worst. We were not long in finding out. When the breathless driver came up, he told us between gasps, that disaster had befallen the herd. It seems they were driving the animals across the frozen estuary of the river when the ice collapsed. How many deer had been lost he didn't know yet. But he needed volunteers to get them out. I immediately called a meeting of the company, which was attended by every deer owner in the village. In very few minutes, we had decided on a course of action. We would go to the herds at once, prepared to stay and do whatever there was to do. This was the one meeting that I attended in which the Eskimos came to a decision without having to sleep on it, proving that they could act swiftly in an emergency.

It was eight miles across glare ice to the mouth of the Arctic River where the accident had occurred. When we got there we were surprised to find that the ice that had broken was sixteen inches thick. But there was no water beneath it so, in effect, it was a bridge of ice that had collapsed. The deer had fallen through to dry ground but had been smothered or trampled to death by the hundreds of scared deer that followed.

Most of the carcasses were already frozen stiff, but others that had been protected by the bodies of those on top, were still warm enough to skin and butcher. We started a fire and on it warmed several buckets of water. Then I had some boys cut off the ears of every deer that had perished. These ears I put into water until they thawed out so that I could read the ear marks. In this way we ascertained ownership of the individual deer.

In the meanwhile, all the carcasses had been recovered and stacked along the river bank. There were 196 of them in all. About a quarter of them were skinned and dressed and cached under the hides. The rest I told the owners to drag to their trap-lines as soon as possible and set their traps around them. One might wonder why I had to tell them this but the reason was that there was a rule against using reindeer meat for bait and the trappers would have observed the rule even in a disaster of this kind. At that time, one could buy a prime reindeer steer for ten dollars so I felt that if they caught only one fox per carcass it would be a good sale. Actually, they averaged a catch of four foxes per carcass and that winter's catch was the greatest in the history of the village. So the disaster to the herd actually turned out to be most profitable to all concerned, for the man who lost the most deer had the most bait and caught the most foxes. Still, recalling the *Dissertation on Roast Pig,* I wondered if in the future years that similar disasters might not overtake the herds about the opening of the trapping season.

Chapter XIV

THE WRECK OF THE SILVERWAVE

We had hardly gotten the deer troubles out of our hair when news of an even greater catastrophe filtered through to us by way of the mukluk telegraph. The mailboat which operated between Nome and Kotzebue, the *Silverwave*, was overdue in Kotzebue and presumed lost somewhere north of Shishmaref. Then a dog-team came in from Wales and confirmed the rumors. The *Silverwave* was indeed lost and Lomen Brothers, who owned it, were arranging for beacon fires to be lit along the coast every ten miles in the hopes that they might aid the survivors, if any, in reaching shore.

It seems ice had prevented the ship from reaching Kotzebue so the skipper, Captain John Hegness, had landed some miles distant and carried the mail bag in to town. But when he returned to the place where he had left the ship, it was nowhere to be seen. Believing it had gotten into a blind lead in the ice pack and was being carried north, Hegness returned to Kotzebue, secured a dogteam, and headed up the coast towards Kivalina hoping to intercept it. In the meanwhile, the mate had blundered into a blind lead and was hopelessly trapped. But, instead of drifting north as Hegness had expected, it headed out then drifted southward. Eventually the pack grounded near Cape Espenberg about seventy-five miles north of Shishmaref. The crew and passengers made shore by spreading planks on the ice, which as yet was unconsolidated. The main party headed back towards Deering, the nearest white community, while the others headed south towards Shishmaref.

But one of the passengers, an old prospector by the name of William Armstrong, took off for an Eskimo camp which he knew to be in the vicinity. Luckily, he found the camp of *Muk-kiak-tuk,* a well-known character of those parts, and engaged him to go back to the ship and rescue the mail. For this service, he promised Mukkiaktuk he could have anything he could salvage from the ship, since it had been abandoned. The Eskimo got the mail off and in addition, several sled loads of loot before the ice parted and the ship went down. Then, according to his agreement, he transported Armstrong and the rescued mail to Shishmaref, a distance of some seventy-five miles, and left Armstrong with us. The old man was pretty well done in from his experience and hardships of the trail, so we decided to keep him until we felt he was again strong enough for travelling, whereupon he would continue on to Nome, his original destination.

In the meanwhile, the other crewmen and passengers began to straggle into the village, having been rescued by local Eskimos who had gone out in search of them. Then began an interesting hassle. The mate who had gotten the ship into trouble in the first place, and who had abandoned it in the ice, and who had failed even to rescue the mail, now learned that Armstrong had it. He tried to recover it by any means short of using a gun, but the old prospector was stubborn. The mail had been abandoned, he had rescued it, so he was going to have the honor of bringing it in to Nome. And that was that.

Some days later, when Armstrong had recovered and we undertook to engage a driver to carry him and the mail to Wales, the first leg of the journey to Nome, one by one our prospects backed out. It was some time before we began to realize that the mate and the fox farmer with whom he was staying were interfering. They wanted either possession of the mail or, failing that, to beat Armstrong in to Nome with their version of the wreck, and why the mail had been abandoned.

One evening a team came in from the direction of Wales and before anyone north of us knew of it, I offered the driver a hundred dollars if he would turn around and go back early the following morning. The price being too good to resist, he accepted the offer. To be certain that nothing would happen to our plans this time we pledged him to absolute secrecy about the trip.

Early next morning Armstrong got away and it was several hours before the news of his departure filtered through to the fox farm. The mate was furious and took after him as soon as he could get away. It looked as if their intentions were to waylay him on the trail and take the mail away from him. But they never caught up, and Armstrong bore the mail triumphantly in to Nome. And shortly thereafter the Lomen Brothers reimbursed me for the hundred dollars I had put up to help Armstrong get the mail through.

We have often wondered what became of Armstrong, although we realize he was old then and suffering from tuberculosis. He probably did not live long after the incident. Someone told us he had been mentioned in "The Spoilers" as a miner who had defended his claim from jumpers with a six-shooter, some twenty-odd years earlier. He had not mentioned that to us but we did learn in a roundabout way that he was a Spanish-American War veteran and that he was somewhat of an inventor, having patented a dummy that was used in the training of prizefighters.

One day when Armstrong was feeling particularly low he told us he had located a couple gold claims on the Imnachuck river that were very rich and he wanted to give them to us since he didn't think he'd live to develop them. One he had named the "Old Soldier" claim for himself and the other the "Dummy" claim for his invention. He had a moosehide poke tied about his waist that was full of nuggets and coarse gold that he said came from these two claims. He shook the gold out on the table one day and urged us to help ourselves. Of course we didn't want any of his gold but he insisted, so we picked out four nuggets worth about fifty cents apiece to remember him by. We still have them but we never investigated the claims. We learned that the paystreak on the Imnachuck was lost when it was crossed by a lava flow and Armstrong professed to have found it again on the far side of the flow and had located his claims there. But they were in permafrost and a shaft to the bedrock where the gold lay would have to be thawed all the way with coal at seventy-five dollars a ton. So we threw the claims over our collective left shoulder and stuck to our schoolteaching. In the years that have passed I have often wondered if Armstrong ever recorded those claims and what became of them. For if he didn't they may still be there untouched these forty years holding a fortune for some enterprising miner with the capital and guts to sink a shaft to bedrock.

Chapter XV

OLD TIMES AND OLDTIMERS

We were now well into our second winter in Shishmaref and were beginning to feel we belonged. Most of the active men were busy with their trapping but the old grandpas were still around and liked to squat around on our floor and tell us about the good old days. They always referred to the bygone days as the *Old Nation* in contradistinction to present times which they called the *New Nation*. And in spite of its small population which perhaps was never any larger, Shishmaref was as true a nation as Andorra or Monaco or any other of the miniscule principalities of the world. For the 3000 odd square miles which comprised its hunting, trapping and fishing grounds were never challenged by any other group and Shishmaref owed no allegiance to any chief or king, paid no taxes, tithes or tribute to anyone in the world.

Life in the *old nation* revolved around an institution called the *kazhgie* locally, although the name is generally applied to the building which housed the institution. But one belonged to a kazhgie like one belongs to a church. If there were several kazhgies in a single large village you would belong to the one to which your father belonged and your son would follow you. Shishmaref had had two kazhgies, one at either end of the village. They were larger than ordinary igloos and from the looks of the ruins they had been circular. Some kazhgies had been heated by central fireplaces in which driftwood was burned but in those at Shishmaref, seal oil had been burned in large stone lamps since driftwood was scarce.

Old men, who had no other home, lived at the kazhgie permanently. Family men worked and ate there, too, their wives carrying food to them, but they slept at home at nights. Adolescent boys could also live at the kazhgie and generally did although they were not compelled to if they would rather live at home. If a boy did move to the kazhgie he would stay there until he married.

To an old man, the kazhgie was something of an old folks home. To the active men it was a club and shop and to the boys it was school. An old man would recite the tribal history, the tales of the heroes and the powerful medicine men or *shamans*, or *angekoks*, locally, and the boys were required to listen and remember. In order that the stories would not change in the telling, each storyteller was flanked by two prompters who set him aright if he made a mistake.

When the men worked, the boys watched, and the merits of a particular design or pattern for a harpoon or some other object was explained to them. Then they would work under the men's supervision. But after the lectures and the manual training classes were over the boys were free to wrestle or dance or engage in various athletic contests.

On other occasions, the whole village would gather in the kazhgie for a feast or for dancing. And then, on more sober occasions, the kazhgie became a courtroom. If someone was causing trouble, the graybeards would discuss the matter at length and finally come up with a verdict. They made no pretense at enforcing their verdicts but as a rule the active men carried them out. Punishments for minor offenses like infidelity might be mere reprimands delivered publicly. Graver offenses would be punished by banishment from the village, either temporary or permanent. But for serious crime like murder they would invoke the death penalty. There were stories of murderers struck from all sides with so many spears that their bodies could not fall to the ground.

In the old nation, to be eligible for marriage, a young man had first to prove his ability as a hunter. He would have to take each of the larger animals such as caribou, polar bear, walrus, oogruk and seal. In addition he would be required to know how to make all his weapons, tools, boats and sleds. Furthermore, he had to be financially able to present his intended bride with a parka.

The girls received no kazhgie training but were trained at home by their own mothers. Before they were eligible for marriage they must know how to make thread, prepare skins and furs for clothing, how to make mukluks, water boots, rain parkas, fur parkas, skin trousers and sleeping bags. In fact, a girl must be able to produce every item the family would ever wear. In addition, besides her cooking and sewing, she would be required to process for winter use everything her husband would bring home from the hunt. Her own contribution to the family larder would be all the vegetable food such as berries, roots, leaves and flowers which she would be expected to gather in great quantities for winter consumption. And all winter, in her spare time, she would fish through the ice for tomcod.

There was no wedding ceremony in the old days. If a young man was interested in a certain girl he would hang around her igloo and help her father whenever he had the chance. Sooner or later, if acceptable to the family, he would be invited to spend the night. Sometime during the night he would attempt to share the berth of his intended bride. According to usage, on the first two or three attempts she would shove him out. But on the fourth try he would be allowed to remain and this acceptance as a bed-mate constituted the marriage.

The young couple would continue to live with the bride's parents until after the second child was born, whereupon the young man would build an igloo of his own. In the meanwhile, the grandparents claimed the grandchildren and looked after them as their own. And the children called their grandparents, mother and father. They still do. Eventually, however, the pendulum would swing and the young couple would become heads of the family and the grandparents would go into well-earned retirement to be looked after in their daughter's home until the end.

There was no rule or restriction against plural wives or even plural husbands in the old nation. In fact, it was an honor for a man to have more than one wife since this would imply that he was a great hunter and brought in more game than one woman could handle. There are stories wherein an overworked house-wife would implore her husband to marry another woman since there was too much work for one. There are also old stories of times when women were in such short supply that several brothers were obliged to share the same wife.

In the old days the hunting of big game such as caribou, bear and whale was done co-operatively, yet certain benefits ac-crued to the man with the sharpest eyes, the best stalker, etc. For instance, the skin of a polar bear belonged to the first man to see the bear, regardless of who killed it. The meat would be divided equally among those in the party. If a whale was caught in a particular man's section of a community net, that man would receive the flukes and a choice section of the back. Or if an oogruk was killed early in the season before the main run was on, it was divided up, the owner receiving the hide and a portion of the meat. Many of the customs of the old days were still in force although introduction of firearms has made men more independent of each other, and the opportunity to sell furs to the outside world has raised the economic level of the village, more or less ending the practice of dividing up and sharing catches, and its attendant social security.

Like people the world over who love to talk about the good old days there is probably not an Eskimo who would be willing to return to them, either, if offered the chance. He would not want to trade his rifle for a harpoon or his Lang stove for a seal oil lamp. It would be hard to get along without steel traps or a *Primus* stove. Or tea and pilot bread and above all, matches. In fact one old fellow solemnly assured me that he could not go long without *kopsetah* (sugar).

The Lang stove had been invented by a Nome man for use by prospectors, but immediately proved a boon to all arctic dwellers including the original inhabitants. It was simply a small box-like sheet-iron stove with an oven. But it had a patented draft which made it possible to hold a fire with no better fuel than a bundle of grass or green willow twigs. And since the draft was directed around the oven, it was an excellent stove for baking bread or roasting meat.

The *Primus* stove was an import from Sweden and was generally referred to as a "Swede stove." It consisted of a pressurized kerosene font and blow torch-like burner. One could make coffee on it in five minutes. It was as foolproof as a Lang stove and nobody in the Arctic in those days would be without one.

Sometimes the old men would entertain us with stories of their own experiences especially of the changing times that began when they were young. There was Okie, for instance, who came in one day and asked me to write a letter to Uncle Sam for him, requesting a pair of glasses. Then he proceeded to tell me how it was that he came to be buddy-buddy with Uncle Sam. A long time ago a white man had come to the village, and the natives had discovered that he had a jug of whiskey on his sled. But the white man wouldn't share it with them under any circumstances. Afraid that they would attempt to steal it from him in the night, the white man decided not to spend the night there as he had originally planned, but continued up the coast where there was a vacant igloo in which he could camp. A short time after he departed a young Eskimo took after him and the rumor spread that he intended to kill the man for his whiskey. When Okie heard this he was worried, for he knew that if the white man was murdered other white men would come and the whole village would be punished for what this one man had done, alone. So Okie hooked up his dogs and took after the Eskimo, hoping he could get there in time to prevent a tragedy. But no, when he arrived at the lone igloo he saw at once that he had come too late. The white man lay dead on the floor and in the corner with the jug between his legs lay the Eskimo, dead drunk. Okie's mind was made up and he wasted no time. Picking up the rifle he shot his townsman dead then returned to the village to await the breakup.

When the ice finally went out and the Revenue Cutter *Bear* hove into sight Okie got in his kayak and paddled out to the ship. To the captain, Okie told the story from beginning to end, hoping thereby to save the village from punishment for the white man's murder by a local Eskimo. When he had finished the captain said, "Okie, that's all right for this time. But next time, *rope* (and here Okie made a circle around his neck), zip! (and here he whistled) . . . pretty soon, no more Okie!"

Another village character who was different from any other Eskimo I had ever seen was Adam Tukoquina. Adam was just plain lazy, not sick or crippled, or too old to work, but just a born panhandler. Whenever white people came to town Adam always showed up with his exhibit number one. Up near Cape Espenberg he had found an outcrop of lignite and had gathered up a sample. This he carried about in a paper bag and showed to every stranger, regardless of his business or calling. His story was always the same. In effect, he wanted Uncle Sam to go up there and start a coal mine and give Adam the proceeds. I was told that Adam had dedicated his life to the promotion of his coal mine but that he had never lifted a pick himself to see if there actually was any coal there.

One spring Adam came to me to get me to buy his house for fifteen dollars. Trying to recall which igloo was his, I came to the conclusion that he didn't have any. But then he and his wife, Eve, and little Cain lived somewhere so I followed Adam through the village to the far end to see where. What he showed me was not an igloo but a cave. He had dug into a sand dune after it had frozen stiff enough to stand up and had spent the winter holed up in it. Now the old fox was trying to sell it to me before it thawed out and collapsed.

Sometime later Adam talked me out of some wooden packing boxes and crates, saying that he needed the material to build a boat. I saw him sitting on the ground beside the pile of boxes, methodically taking them apart and saving the nails and boards, none of which was more than a yard long. Then I forgot all about him, as his project of merely taking the boxes apart and straightening the nails promised to last him all summer. But some months later when Toni and I crossed the channel to the next island north, we came upon Adam's boat where he had cached it after making the channel crossing. How he and his family ever made it in that leaky cockle shell made of cull quarter-inch pine box boards and with box nails, I'll never know, for it wouldn't have been safe in a bath tub.

Another interesting character was Poosruk and that would go for his entire family and dog team. They were all so poor and scrawny one would think they were starving to death but that was not the case as there was always plenty of native food in Shishmaref. It may be that they were afflicted by some unusual disease for they seemed to be without energy. Poosruk walked so slowly that you would wonder if he would be able to lift his foot again for the next step. And his dogs were just like him, perhaps from habit and example. I remember seeing him set off across the lagoon just at daybreak, walking like he was going to his own hanging. When the sun set that brief winter day he was still in sight since none of his dogs had ever learned to trot, either.

Poosruk had no boys but there were three or four girls. All were skinny, hollow-cheeked and ugly by any standard. The entire family dressed in cloth parkas made of striped mattress ticking. These garments were made with the stripes running up and down. If there was any fur beneath them it must have been extremely thin as it didn't show even at the edges. To see this hooded, striped, lean and gaunt family huddled around a campfire behind a sand dune one would think he had come upon an Arab camp deep in the Sahara.

The women were harder to get acquainted with than the men, since most of them spoke not a word of English and we knew less Innuit. But through those with whom we could converse, we learned much of the current gossip and what was going on between these good women. Probably the biggest hassle of all was the one going on between Mrs. Cross Nonock and Mrs. Billy Atatayák. Mrs. Cross, as they usually called her, believed that cleanliness was far ahead of Godliness and she was a pious woman. Her igloo was as neat as a pin at all times. Poor old Cross, her more or less henpecked husband, was considerably handicapped by her ideas. I remember seeing him carving something of wood one day, and carefully dropping each individual shaving in a tomato can on the floor beside him while Mrs. Cross sat opposite watching his every move.

Mrs. Atatayák was quite the opposite. Her igloo smelled to high heaven at all times and she and her large brood matched their surroundings. I doubt that any of them had ever been clean. The argument between the two women was how to raise children, clean or dirty. Mrs. Atatayák argued that they should be brought up filthy, and the filthier, the better. She practiced her belief and as proof of the soundness of her theory she had borne nine children, all apparently healthy, and she had never lost one. Poor Mrs. Cross, for all her immaculate housekeeping and modern theories on sanitation, didn't have a leg to stand on. She had never raised a child!

In spite of the apparent truth in Mrs. Atatayák's logic, the village women had organized, probably at some schoolteacher's instigation, and periodically inspected each igloo. Any igloo that didn't pass inspection was posted. I recall going up the village street one day and seeing a wrathy woman glaring at a sheet of paper stuck to the wall of her igloo and obviously cursing in Innuit. The sign stated, rather bluntly, I thought, "This House is Dirty." But the outraged housewife left it there. What sanctions they could impose, I do not know, but the only way to get rid of the sign was to clean house.

Actually we often wondered how those Eskimo women kept their houses as clean as they did, but probably what helped most was the fact that about all one could track in would be dry snow, and at the very worst, clean sand. Yet they were one-roomed igloos and everything had to be done in that one room for at least eight months of the year. This included skinning seals oozing blood and oil, plucking birds, cooking, eating, sleeping, making skin and fur garments, carving wood, bone, ivory and antler.

To give an idea of the sizes of these igloos, Tingook's was 10 feet by 14 feet with five-foot walls and a gable six and one-half feet high. Four people slept there. Sublook's was 12 feet by 16 feet with six-foot walls and eight-foot gable. Eight people slept in this room regularly. Allockeok's was eight feet by 13 feet with six-foot walls and ceiling. Six people slept there, three adults and three children. Tocktoo, the man with two wives, had the biggest igloo. It was a palatial 15 feet by 16 feet with six-foot walls and seven and three-quarter foot gable, housing ten people at that time.

Of the twenty-five igloos that I measured the average size was 10 feet by 14 feet and the average number of occupants was seven. Each had one gut window in the roof as a rule, although a few had a glazed window in the wall. There was also a ventilator in the roof about four inches square. Furnishings consisted of bunks or sleeping platforms piled with deerskins and sleeping bags under which clothing and duffle was stored, a *Lang* stove, a few pots and pans and dishes, and that was about all. Small children slept in hammocks swung across the rear corners of the room. If the family was relatively well-fixed they had a Coleman gas lamp; if not, an ordinary kerosene wick lamp. A few families still used the old stone seal oil lamps and all of them had them on hand (usually on the roof) stored against the day when they couldn't afford white man's innovations.

What they didn't have in that one room were such space-consuming items as tables and chairs or anything else that could be classed as furniture. Food supplies for immediate use were kept in the storm shed along with other items not in use, but the bulk of the winter stores were kept on a tall cache behind the igloo.

Most of us have heard about *kitchen middens,* those prehistoric garbage heaps so dear to the heart of archaeologists. We saw dozens of them in the making. The Eskimo housewife spends only the freeze-up period in the igloo. So she blithely tosses all refuse out the front and only door. If the pups don't eat it, perhaps the ravens and gulls will; in any event it will soon be covered up by snow, anyway. And being frozen, it is not offensive to the Eskimo nostril, either. Come spring when the snow melts, the garbage thaws and a sour stench arises. But the Eskimo family is then far away, dwelling in a tent on some sandy beach enjoying the sweet air from sea and blooming tundra. In the meanwhile the beach grass around the igloo grows rank from the winter's fertilizing and before fall has covered all the bones, hides, feathers and lost items which a thousand years hence become the precious prehistoric *artifacts* of the archaeologist. When the family returns in the fall the grass, now brown and fallen in tangled mats, has blanketed the past winter's accumulation, elevated the site an iota and the cycle begins anew. Some of these Alaskan village sites are so old and have been occupied for so long that the artifacts found on the bottom are 2000 years old. From studies of them we learn that the Eskimos who first came to Seward Peninsula from Asia were skillful workers in ivory and flint and had a formalized art style vastly superior to any they have had since. How deep the Shishmaref middens are and what lies at the bottom we didn't find out as we did no digging. Somehow, we couldn't bring ourselves to it since the present inhabitants still seemed too closely linked with the past. It would have been like digging in some inhabited village's cemetery. I did dig a hole about six feet deep through a sand dune though, and found permafrost at that level so if the middens extend beyond that depth they are relatively secure against ordinary pothunters and should remain undisturbed until science is ready to take a look.

Chapter XVI

OUR SECOND CHRISTMAS

I had spent our first Christmas in Alaska on the trail, so naturally I looked forward to the second with considerable enthusiasm, particularly since Toni had told me of all the interesting festivities I had missed. This year there would be an additional attraction. We had written our friends and relatives in the states requesting them to send up any outgrown clothing they could scare up. This they had done, and when the *Boxer* arrived the following summer, it had three enormous cases of clothing for us. That fall we had gotten these garments out and the girls in Toni's sewing class had altered them to fit various individuals in our school and village. So, now they were to be distributed as Christmas presents. I'll never forget the looks on the faces of those Eskimo children as they were presented with the first manufactured garments they had ever possessed. Think of it! Children who had never worn anything but hide and hair, fabricated in their own igloo, now receiving a bright woolen sweater or a suit of clothes or a jacket, or a shirt and tie. And the girls getting blouses and skirts for the first time. Even real stockings, hair ribbons and handkerchiefs. The uplift to their little egos must have been terrific. Most of them put on their new garments at once and all evening we noticed them running their hands over the cloth and looking at their finery with obvious pride and satisfaction.

The day following the school program, the village council took over the schoolhouse in preparation for the full week's festivities, which always occupied the week between Christmas Day and New Year's Day. All the desks and other furniture were removed from the little 25 by 30 foot schoolroom and stored in the coalshed. By sitting on the floor, and practically in each other's laps, everybody in the village could gain access and did unless bedfast. The program began with a feast—not a banquet or community dinner. Only *feast* could describe the repast adequately. For what might have been lacking in quality was more than made up in quantity. They brought in tubs and wash boilers of seal, reindeer, and oogruk meat, fish and wildfowl, either boiled, roasted, raw, dry or frozen. In came sealskin pokes of berries frozen in seal oil and other pokes of grated and frozen willow leaves and lousewort flowers. For dessert, they had gallons of *aukootuk* and *kummommuk,* two varieties of Eskimo ice cream concocted of snow, tallow, seal oil and dried berries. Except for the pilot bread and tea, white man's foods were absent.

Immediately after the feast, a reindeer sledge race was held, to take advantage of what little daylight there was. Even then it was held in semi-darkness since the sun is up only an hour and a half during the Christmas holidays. The race was run on a ten-mile triangular course so that the participants could be seen at all stages of the race. After it was over, everybody went home except the council which returned to the schoolhouse. There it decided on the prizes to be given to the winners of this day's events and prepared the schedule of events for the morrow. When everything was settled they rang the school bell and the villagers reassembled in the schoolhouse. The village president thereupon arose and announced the day's winners and the program for the following day. Then the winners and the losers, too, were called forward to receive their awards. Village belles then stepped forward by prearrangement and placed ribbons on the winners. Then came the prizes. These did not issue from the council or committee but from anyone who felt so inclined. And the prizes did not go to the winners, necessarily. A popular loser might conceivably receive more prizes than the winner. Each gift had a loop attached to it that was put around the recipient's neck. Months must have gone into the preparation of these gifts for we saw them give fancy mukluks, dog and reindeer harness, coils of oogruk skin lashing, sealskins, fish, seals, reindeer skins, parkas, slippers and even store-bought items like rifles, shotguns and traps.

In most instances the gifts were presented by the women who made them. And the man would reciprocate with a small gift from the store such as a bottle of perfume, a necklace, handkerchiefs, soap or chewing gum, always presented with an appropriate humorous remark which would set the receiver as well as the audience laughing uproariously.

But people who had not entered the race might be called up to receive a gift, often as a joke. We saw a childless young couple presented with a doll which they received with red faces, and an unlucky hunter given a polar bear's paw; another, a seal pup. An old miner from the Kougarok happened to be in town to purchase dog feed and was invited to the celebration. During the course of the evening someone placed a sealskin noose around his neck and told him to pull in the line which ran through the crowd and out the door. The old man began pulling and soon a large coil of valuable lashing lay at his feet. Something heavy was at the other end of the line and as it slithered through the door peals of laughter erupted from the crowd. The old miner finally reeled in a frozen seal which, with the lashing, was a very useful present to him.

When all of the gifts had been distributed, two men were chosen to represent two opposite sides into which the populace was then divided. These teams competed against each other in athletic events every evening thereafter until New Year's Eve. The least difficult trials came first and were participated in by the younger members of the teams. The first was a test of finger strength. The two contestants sat facing each other, each with a leg over and a leg under those of his opponent. Fingers were locked at the second joint and the test began. One took a position with his arm held close to his chest while the other with arm extended, tried to pull it away. If he failed, they reversed positions and kept at it until one acknowledged defeat.

The arm test followed, the contestants assuming the same position as in the finger test but with their arms locked at the wrists. Then came the pushing test. The opponents sat on the floor, back to back, palms of hands flat on the floor. There was no mark or line or distance one had to push the other to win. It simply continued like the contests preceding it until one or the other considered himself bested. He would then give an exclamation of surprise and wonder in appreciation of the other's skill or strength and get up and go to the loser's bench with a smile.

Two types of wrestling followed without benefit of a wrestling mat of any sort. In the first, the opponents knelt, took shoulder holds and endeavored to toss the other over his head. The other was the well-known Indian style wrestling wherein the contestants laid flat on their backs, feet to head, raising the right leg three times and crossing them in the third to come down with a swift motion designed to lift and throw the opponent.

Following the wrestling matches came hand walking contests. In this remarkable feat, the body was held horizontal to the floor, elevated about four inches above it. Most of us would find it impossible even to assume the position let alone walk, but these boys were able to take a dozen or more steps (on their hands) in this position.

Still more difficult was the kneeling kick. From a kneeling position, in one movement the contestant comes to a squatting position and with both feet, kicks a ball suspended on a string before him, and land on his feet. Some of the young athletes were able to kick a ball in this manner that was suspended two feet above the floor.

In the next contest the same type of kick was made from a standing position, the feet being held together and striking a ball dangling above their heads, after which the contestants landed on their feet.

Following the wrestling and kicking contests, a slack rope was put up from wall to wall and a number of tests were conducted thereon. These contests were repeated each evening all week except the one night devoted to women's contests. We were told that all of these contests were part of a warrior's training of long ago. On the eve of battle any man who would fail in these trials was disqualified as a fighter and sent back to camp in disgrace.

The women's contests were not designed to train warriors, but for escape. Whether it was escape from a Siberian invader or an amorous swain was beside the point. Girls and women habitually work cutting up fish and seals, bent double. They had to be able to leap up from this quasi-squatting position and land, running. So they had squat-jump contests and foot races. Several of the more comely girls had become quite expert from practice.

The afternoon events were dogteam races for men, women and boys, and foot races for various classes from three-year-olds up. There were no dashes. The nearest thing was the race for the three-year-olds which was about two hundred yards. Girls from nine to twelve ran a two-mile race and young men, five miles.

On the last day of the year another feast was held, nearly on the same lavish scale as at Christmas. This was followed by prize giving and the annual election. The remaining time until midnight was spent in story-telling. Just before the stroke of twelve, the men and boys stepped out for their rifles and shotguns which were waiting loaded, and the New Year was greeted by a deafening bombardment that kept up for an hour. The celebration was over.

Next morning there was a general exodus from the village. Dogteams could be seen going out in every direction. Some men were going for wood; others to their traplines. And still others were returning to the herds with their families after a wonderful week on the coast with friends and relatives.

Chapter XVII

A WANDERER ON THE ICE

Sometime after the new year when the days began to lengthen and the hunters and trappers went abroad more, we began to hear rumors of a lost man being sighted near the village. Apparently a hunter had seen strange footprints on the sea ice and had reported it. Later, another hunter had seen a man on the ice afoot, and had tried to go to him but the stranger had fled out to sea again. I was interested, naturally, and wondered why the man had avoided the hunter. Discussing it with the hunters I soon found that this was old stuff with them and that lost men always followed a similar pattern of behavior. A hunter lost on the ice drifts into unknown coasts where men might be hostile and would kill him. Therefore they try to get back into familiar territory without being observed. This seemed to make sense even in our time for an Eskimo could conceivably land in Siberia unbeknown to himself because of darkness or fog. In fact, one of our boys did drift over to the Siberian coast and was given up for lost. But another wind brought him home again. Alas, his wife had already remarried. He, however, did not feel she had waited long enough before remarrying, so to punish her he bit off her nose.

The detective work these Eskimos did in this particular incident would have done credit to Scotland Yard. They knew he was lost because he had retreated out to sea when he smelled smoke. They knew he was very weak because his footprints were close together. He was a stranger from afar because his mukluk print was of an unfamiliar type. Then the tracks headed southwest and we heard no more of the lost one for a time.

One night I was up at Percy Blatchford's place visiting. Percy, I should have mentioned before, was an Englishman married to a pretty Eskimo girl. It was he who had been pen-raising white foxes against the day when the fox farmer would arrive with blue foxes to cross with them. He had a trading outfit, also, and his place was quite a hangout for a number of young and unattached boys. Anyway, while we were visiting, a racket was heard in the stormshed and Percy sent a boy out to see what was up. Presently the boy returned and said someone had taken a pair of mukluks from the stormshed. The next morning, day-

light revealed the tracks of the lost man coming in from the
north and retreating in the same direction. No attempt was made
to follow the tracks or to retrieve the missing mukluks. In fact,
just the opposite course was taken. People throughout the village
began putting out food and clothing that the lost man might
easily find and take without showing himself. The strategy
worked as the tracks returned to the village for several days and
some of the items left for the lost man were taken. Then one day
the tracks took off up the coast, heading north, and were seen
no more in the village or its vicinity.

In the meanwhile trapping season had closed and one day
a couple of our boys took off for Deering on their annual fur-
selling and visiting spree. A short distance out of Deering was a
lone igloo where they planned to spend the night so they could
arrive in Deering fresh. But upon arriving at the place they could
see by tracks and other sign that the igloo was occupied although
no dog or sledge tracks could be seen. It was quite dark but the
boys had a flashlight and when they flashed it in the igloo, someone in there begged them to turn it off, saying he couldn't stand
the light. But they had seen that he was an Eskimo like themselves and speaking their language, however with a strange
dialect. After they were settled for the night, the stranger told
them his story. Several months earlier, he didn't know how long
ago it was, he had been out on the sea ice near Wainwright
hunting polar bear. He had already killed one and was in pursuit
of the second. In the excitement of the chase he had neglected
to watch the ice and it had broken off, setting him adrift. Seeing
that he couldn't get ashore he went back to his kill and filled his
pack sack with meat. Then he started walking. He walked, and
the ice pack drifted for many days, during which time he didn't
see land once. Then he saw a mountain which, from his description of it, must have been Devil Mountain near Cape Espenberg.
The ice continued drifting in a southerly direction and several
days later he saw a man on the ice but ran away from him because he was afraid the man might kill him. Then one day the
ice grounded and he nearly got ashore but he smelled smoke and
went out to sea again as he thought the people there might be
hostile. About twenty-five miles farther south he was near shore
again when he saw two men kill a polar bear on the ice. He
waited until the men had left and then went ashore at that place.
There was an igloo there and a cache and from this place he
bought some matches and a tin can. These he needed to melt

snow for drinking water. He was never hungry, he said, but always was thirsty because there was salt in the sea ice that he had been forced to use for water.

From this point he started north again and presently came to a large village. Here, he said, he *bought* a pair of mukluks and some food. He gave the boys his name and asked them to notify the people he had *bought* things from, that he would pay for them, cash or trade. An Eskimo, who would not borrow or steal, could *buy* without benefit of a *seller*.

Whether he ever got back to Wainwright again we never learned but he was 500 miles from home when he got ashore. So far as we could tell his story was true for two of our men had killed a polar bear at Sinoset, 25 miles south of Shishmaref just about the time the lost man was there.

Chapter XVIII

A SCHOOLMAN DIES

On March three we received word that the Wales schoolmaster, Mr. King, had died suddenly. Since he and his wife were the only white people in that village I thought it would be only neighborly for me to go down there to see if there was anything I could do.

We had not met the Kings since they had come in only the past summer. But we had had correspondence with them on matters of mutual interest and had come to the conclusion that they were more of the nature of missionaries than school people. Every letter we received from them closed with "Yours at His feet" or "Yours in Jesus Christ" or other similar phrases. Not being of a very religious nature, much less devout, my letters must have left them cold. Anyway, we took off the following morning and had a good trip until we reached Mitliktavik, about a dozen miles from Wales. Here we encountered a howling blizzard which we decided not to tackle until the following morning. But the morning found a hurricane blowing, nothing being visible but a whirling mass of snow and icy particles. We took off anyway and got into Wales sometime in the early afternoon. Nayokpuk, my driver, put up with a friend at the edge of the village and I walked on to the schoolhouse expecting to be put up there. However, when I beat on the heavy door someone eventually came, opened the door a crack, and inquired who I was and what was my business. I introduced myself whereupon the good lady said, "Well, in that case, I guess you can come in."

I entered and confronted my hostess, a rather dowdy woman of middle age, and an Eskimo girl. I then told her I had heard of the loss of her husband and had come to see if I could be of any assistance in her time of sorrow. Yes, she said, there was something I could do for her. Mr. King had always done the clerical work and she knew nothing about preparing the reports that the Bureau of Education required of each station. I thereupon assured her that I would be glad to show her how to make them. Then I asked her if it would be possible for me to stay in the schoolhouse while I was in town since there was no other accommodation available. Reluctantly, she said it would be all right since Frank Martin, the fur buyer from Nome, had stopped there the night before. But, she added regretfully, she couldn't charge me for the room since it was Government property. Then she told me where the room was, where I would find some blankets and where the coal bin was. I went upstairs to the room, cold as Greenland, found the box of blankets and made up the bed. Then I took the coal hod and went downstairs and filled it. When I returned and opened the pot-bellied stove to build a fire I was surprised to find in it, a large sardine tin, freshly opened. That didn't look good to me, at all.

Sometime around four p.m. Mrs. King called up to me saying they were going to sing hymns and have prayers, and didn't I want to join them. Not being able to sing a note, I had a good reason to decline, whereupon Mrs. King said they would pray for me. They might have at that but I didn't stay for the services.

An hour or so later, Mrs. King called up again saying that they were going to have dinner and asked me if I had a grub box. I said I did but that it was at the other end of the village, where-upon I was invited to dinner. I came down to the kitchen where the table was set. While a lengthy grace was being said, I eyed the table, since I hadn't eaten since early morning and was famished. There was one large potato and one small piece of meat. The meat baffled me. There was reindeer hair on it but I was certain that it wasn't reindeer meat.

After the grace, my hostess picked up a knife, looked down the blade like a rifle barrel and very carefully cut the potato into three equal parts. She took the first and laid it in her plate, the Eskimo girl got the second and I came in possession of the third. Then she asked me what I wanted to drink. "Oh, I drink any-thing," I said airily, whereupon Mrs. King said, "Well, we drink water but you can have tea if you wish." I wished tea because it would be warm, I hoped, and maybe I'd get a lump of sugar. Then, out of the blue, "Do you like polar bear meat?" As hungry as I was I said, "No, thank you," on account of the reindeer hair and not just because polar bear meat tastes like a boar hog that had been fattened on dog salmon.

That was it, tea and potato, and then I knew why the sardine tin was in the stove upstairs. Several months later in Nome I mentioned the tin to Frank Martin and he blew his gaskets. He also cleared up the mystery of the reindeer hair on the polar bear meat. It had been offered to him the day before and when he declined it, Mrs. King had put it under the stove for the cat. Apparently it had been retrieved for me when the cat had turned it down. I never did find out who finally ate it but I'm sure it wasn't wasted in that household. Later that evening I worked my way through the blizzard to the igloo at the edge of the village and ate from my grub box.

There were compensations, though, for it was there that I first learned the cause of the schoolmaster's death. It seems, Mr. King was something of a health faddist. And finding himself in failing health he had resorted to a formula that had worked once before but probably wasn't exactly designed for the Cape Prince of Wales climate.

The schoolhouse sat near the beach at the foot of Wales mountain. During the winter, winds of hurricane force come down the mountainside and whirl about the schoolhouse. This causes the snow to build up like a wall around the building, yet leaving an area completely bare between the wall and the build- ing like an arena, in the center of which was the schoolhouse. In this secluded area, Mr. King took to racing round and round the schoolhouse, completely nude, save for a pair of moccasins which he wore to protect his feet from the gravel. Even a strong heart might have failed under such drastic treatment. The natives buried the body in the village cemetery a short distance from the schoolhouse. They were given a coffee can of dry beans for their pains, which they told me they regarded as very poor pay con- sidering the deep snow, the frozen topsoil and the permafrost underneath.

The following morning I attempted to show Mrs. King how to do the *clerical work*. I found the school register had never been kept or even opened and no reports had as yet been mailed in to the Seattle Office of the Bureau of Education. But records of a sort had been kept on tablet paper and were hanging on nails on the wall, one nail for each month. From these attendance records I was able to open the register, compute the percentages and averages required for the record and endeavored to teach Mrs. King how to carry on. It was hopeless, though. I soon found she could not do fourth grade arithmetic and had never heard of percentage or decimal fractions. So I made up her reports and records through February and trusted someone else would come by to help out on the two remaining months of the school year.

We left Wales early the next morning in the same howling blizzard that had greeted us three days before. We knew, though, that the farther we got away from Wales Mountain the better the weather would be. We missed Mitliktavik entirely and emerged from the storm in unfamiliar surroundings. But presently the dogs began turning their noses to the right and sniffing the air in that direction. This concerted sniffing may mean any one of several things. Sometimes it indicates the presence nearby of a trapped fox. Other times it reveals the proximity of a reindeer herd. And sometimes it means a human habitation. Nayokpuk swung the team around and let the dogs follow their noses, which they did with gusto. A short time later we saw a short, steaming ventilator rising above a snowy mound, and several dug-in and tethered dogs lifted their heads to sniff the air at our approach.

Chapter XIX

A NIGHT WITH THE CAVEMEN

While Nayokpuk was occupied staking our dogs to convenient niggerheads, I went over to the igloo from which no one had emerged as yet. The entrance was narrow and low, so low in fact that I had to crawl in and through the long passage leading to the inner door. After I had crawled some twelve or fifteen feet I came suddenly to a drop-off, which in the absolute darkness stopped me cold. The passageway was too narrow to turn around in, so I had to back all the way out, then re-enter in reverse. When I came again to the drop-off I simply let my legs over the edge and touched a floor about three feet below. At this point there was another tiny door on which I rapped. From within I heard a woman's voice ask, "Kee-nah?" I replied "Es-keok-te," whereupon the voice beyond the door said in broken English, "Koom-een."

Why had she asked "who is it?" Because I had rapped. An Eskimo would have opened the door without knocking. And when I revealed that I was a *schoolteacher* she immediately employed just about all the English she had at her command and invited me in.

The family within was rather hard to figure out since none of them, not even the men, spoke English. Sitting on the floor to the right of the entrance was a woman who must have been past sixty. Beside her was a stone seal oil lamp of semi-lunar form. A wick laid the length of the straight edge was burning with a clear, flickering flame. She was sewing, and held her hands close to the flame, partly to illuminate her work and partly to warm her hands as there was no other source of heat or light in the room. Now and then, when the lamp smoked or burned unevenly she would manipulate the wick with a pencil-like piece of jade kept for this purpose.

On the floor nearby was a little Eskimo girl perhaps four years old. She was playing with a toy sled and dogteam. The sled had been carved from a single piece of wood but the dogs hadn't been carved at all. They were human finger bones, bleached white. No doubt she had found them herself in a nearby burial ground. Just beyond her, sitting on the edge of the sleeping platform, was a man perhaps a little older than the woman, that I took for her husband. He was busy carving another toy for the little girl who was obviously the apple of his eye. I gathered that she was either a grandchild or a gift child since they often have either when they can no longer have children of their own.

These three were typical malemiut Eskimos such as one might encounter anywhere between Unalakleet and Kotzebue. But perched at the rear of the wide sleeping platform was another kind of Eskimo. He was a young man, perhaps in his mid-thirties, large and powerfully built. His face was broad and his nose was wide and low at the root. He had a butcher-knife haircut which gave him heavy bangs at the eyebrows and his complexion was the darkest I had seen in the Arctic. This character was engaged in devouring the raw foreleg of a reindeer, the hoof and a little hide and hair of which was still attached. I sat with my back against the opposite wall smoking my pipe while I watched this fellow at his meal. Sitting there on the floor, looking up at the smoke-blackened ceiling, I felt almost as if I were in a cave and actually watching a caveman at his dinner. It couldn't have been much different 30,000 years ago wherever cavemen hunted reindeer then. This fellow would sink his pearly teeth into the red muscle and tear it loose by jerking back his head. Then while he was chewing up that huge mouthful he would be eyeing the piece in his hands to decide where he would attack it next.

Finally he reached the point when there was nothing left but bone and hoof. Thereupon he drew from his belt a twelve-inch Willson knife and, using the back of it like a hammer, began beating the bone to pieces. Soon he was scooping up the red, oily marrow and eating it with great relish. At last his meal was finished. He looked at the shattered bones and the hoof, turning them over speculatively, then cast them aside. He wiped his hands on his parka, passed his sleeve over his mouth a couple of times and laid down. Drawing his sleeping bag up to his neck he rolled over and was soon sleeping peacefully. The rest of us shortly followed suit. I may have dreamed of cavemen and pleistocene horses and mammoths that night but it was pleasant sleep nonetheless. This little glimpse had taught me that cavemen must have been friendly, hospitable people and not at all wild and savage as we have been so often led to believe.

Morning found us again on the trail and at the end of a long day we smelled the smoke of Shishmaref. Soon we were in our homes and surrounded by the curious to whom every traveler is the bearer of tidings, good or bad. In other words, on that day we were the *mukluk telegraph.*

Chapter XX

A BIRTH IN THE HERDS

Fawning time is one of the critical periods in the life of a reindeer herder and while it varies somewhat, the middle of April will find it at its height in the Seward Peninsula area. About that time, I have forgotten the exact date, I accompanied a large party of deer owners to the Serpentine herds where they were to aid the chief herder and his apprentices during fawning. As we neared the herd we kept flushing large red foxes that had lately taken to prowling around the herds in hopes of carrying off an unattended fawn. They get more than one would suspect for some reindeer, particularly young does having their first fawns, are not good mothers and occasionally abandon their offspring. Others, born weak or rickety, soon fall prey to the marauding foxes and wolves.

I had never discussed fawning with anybody hence the sight that met my eyes gave me the surprise of my life. All the male deer had withdrawn from the females and were grazing on a low hill a mile or so away. But here I was in the center of a herd of some 4000 females all in the act of becoming mothers. Fawns were being dropped by the dozens on all sides. Some dark, some light, some spotted, a few albino. Several of the does needed assistance and were getting it from the deermen. Others were licking their offspring affectionately. Fawns, perhaps minutes old, were steaming in the niggerheads at twenty below zero. One would wonder how any of them could possibly survive a birth which included a sudden drop of environmental temperature of more than a hundred degrees. Yet, percentagewise, survival was very high. Most of the fawns, as soon as they dried off, looked strong and healthy and well adapted to the climate in their woolly fur coats which contrasted strangely with the hairy coats of the adults.

Before nightfall, an unseasonal storm blew up and our entire party had to take refuge in the tiny igloo of the chief herder. He was a young fellow, perhaps about twenty-five, and his wife was a mere girl, sixteen or seventeen years old. Even in her fur parka it was quite obvious that she, too, was about to become a mother.

I doubt that the floor space of the igloo was more than ten

by twelve feet but somehow the fourteen of us found places to spread our sleeping bags when bedtime came. My allotted space was partly under the Lang stove which luckily for me had rather long legs. Its principal disadvantage was that I would be the first one who would have to get up in the morning.

I slept well in spite of the hard bed and cramped quarters but sometime in the middle of the night I heard or imagined I heard an infant crying lustily. I was sure I had seen no child in the igloo that evening and I wondered, half-awake, where it could have been.

Early the next morning I was awakened, as I knew I would be, by the young herder who wanted to build a fire. But I noticed that he was all smiles and quite elated about something. Then I glanced toward the bunk where I saw the reason. His little wife was proudly holding her first born, whose very first cry I had heard during the night. It was almost impossible to believe. Here, this young girl, unattended except by her husband, had crawled out to the stormshed over the bodies of twelve sleeping men, given birth to her baby, and got back to her bed without disturbing anyone. And so far as I could see, all they had to work with was a bag of ptarmigan feathers, a little water, and some seal oil. Mother and baby were doing fine.

Chapter XXI

· TAYLOR CREEK
AND HIBERNATING MEN

We closed school on the thirtieth of April as the villagers
were anxious to leave town and get out to their oogruk camps.
Since we were leaving Shishmaref perhaps never to return we
gave a farewell party for our students. This was a good opportunity to use up a lot of our surplus supplies for we knew mere
cake and pink lemonade would not be considered a party in these
parts. Any white man's food would be acceptable so long as there
would be plenty of it. So we baked gallons of beans and hundreds
of biscuits. And we had oceans of tea with sugar. In addition, we
had side dishes which took care of our oversupply of pickles,
olives, jams and jelly. Our party soon developed into an eating
contest as we had suspected it would. Never had so few eaten
so much so long. But at length the food was gone and one by one
our happy, overstuffed guests thanked us and departed.

The next morning I set off on a trip I had been looking forward to with anticipation for some time. My friend, Allockeok,
had bought a warehouse on Dick Creek in the Kougarok country
some sixty miles inland and I had offered to help him dismantle
it for transportation by dog sledge to the coast. At the end of our
first day's journey we were in a region that afforded no building
material for a shelter except snow so I got to see my first true
snow igloo constructed. It was actually quite a simple feat for
Allockeok as he was in the habit of building them each year on
his trapline. His only tool was a large Willson knife with which
he cut the snow into blocks some eighteen inches square. These
blocks, cut from a deep drift, were feather-light and could be
compared to cinder blocks for construction. The completed igloo
was about seven feet in diameter and about five feet high. For
ventilation I burned a hole through the top with my tundra stove.
Applying the heat, I found that the snowblocks acted like blotters,
sucking up the thawed water so that none dripped down. In fact,
that was one of the chief advantages of the snow house. No matter how warm it was inside, it never dripped. The whole interior
could become smoke blackened but it would remain as dry as
a bone.

When the igloo was finished, Allockeok pitched a fawnskin tent inside for added insulation and we were comfortably established for the night. I have since wished a hundred times that I had a photograph of that igloo because many so-called authorities say the Alaska Eskimos do not and cannot build snow igloos. However, my camera had a habit of freezing up in extremely cold weather and I had not carried it on that trip.

The second day found us at Serpentine Hot Springs near Midnight Mountain on the spine of Seward Peninsula. The gold miners in the district had built a bathhouse with a bunkhouse adjoining so they could take the baths in relative comfort. The springs issued from several places and flowed, steaming, down to a small lake that contained fish and remained open all winter due to the super-heated waters of its only inlet. Several gulls that had arrived about a month early were floating on the lake, perhaps the only open water within hundreds of miles. There was also a patch of open ground, kept free from snow by internal fires, where the miners planted their gardens of cabbage and turnips, some of which were still standing.

The water, as it issued from the ground, was too hot to touch. It contained salt, lime, iron and sulphur, and crystals of these and other minerals could be seen encrusting the grass or clustering, jewellike, on pebbles showing above the water. We found that with the addition of a little pepper, the water made an acceptable consommé.

The bathhouse itself was so full of steam that I could never get a look at it but under foot it felt like plank construction. There were no pipes, but wooden gates could be manipulated to control the flow of hot and cold water. Allockeok and I enjoyed the bath but found we could not stay in long without weakening. He told me the Eskimos had known of the springs and the healing qualities of the water and had bathed there for their health for generations.

The next day we headed for Taylor Creek to visit Tom Chase, the venerable keeper of the roadhouse and long time friend of Allockeok. But enroute we came to a lone log cabin which housed another old friend of Allockeok's. From all appearances the cabin was deserted as no tracks were to be seen in the snow around the place. But Allockeok finally got the door open and we both entered with such caution and respect as one might reserve for the dead. It was quite dark inside as there were no windows and the only light followed us in through the doorway which we partly closed on account of the cold. In one corner I could see an enormous heap of blankets and furs, and in the other a table, chair and stove. The stove was cold and the dishes on the table contained dried-on food that could have been there for weeks.

In the meanwhile, Allockeok had been shouting in the direction of the bed pile and tugging at something in the heap. Eventually there was a stirring that indicated something alive was embedded therein. After some minutes a bewhiskered man kicked himself loose and rolled out, fully clothed. Because of his long, unkempt hair and full beard I may have misjudged his age but I would say he was somewhere in his sixties. He didn't stand up but just sat on the edge of the bunk with his head between his hands, looking at the floor. Allockeok talked to him for some time but to no avail. The man apparently listened but didn't answer. Finally Allockeok gave up and we went out, closing the door securely as we did so. But before the door was closed I noticed the fellow was already crawling under his mound of bedding.

When I commented on the man's strange behavior Allockeok said that it was nothing unusual this time of year. These old miners had been in the hills so long that they had lost all contact with the outside world. They imagined that they had been left behind by progress and could not find work if they did go *outside*. So they had taken to wintering in the Kougarok. Not having any dogs to feed and little or no fuel to burn, they spent days on end in bed. Allockeok compared their situation to that of bears that hole up when food gets scarce and live on their accumulated fat. The conditions for quasi-hibernation certainly were there: darkness, quiet, and a greatly reduced temperature. And from the evidence on the table it was quite likely this old man didn't wake up and eat for weeks at a time.

There were other men in the neighborhood doing the same thing and an outsider would wonder why they didn't pair up and bunk together at least for the companionship. Experience had taught them otherwise. They knew about *cabin fever*, that strange malady of the north wherein even the best of friends come to hate the sight of each other and commit murder for such offenses as drumming on the table or picking one's nose.

That night was spent at the Taylor Creek Roadhouse visiting with Allockeok's long time friend, Tom Chase, who had been in the Kougarok since the first discovery and who was ultimately the source of Allockeok's white man's learning. He certainly was

well read and well informed on the geology and mineralogy of
Seward Peninsula and from him I learned the history of the
Kougarok mining district. I still remember him kindly for the
liniment he gave me for my charley horses as I had gotten quite
lame from the two days' mushing uphill without properly breaking in for it.

Next morning we took off for Dick Creek where the building
stood that we had come up to dismantle. We had not gone far
when we came upon some tracks in the snow, the likes of which
we had never seen before. The dogs took an immediate interest
in them so Allockeok gave them their head and we were off in
pursuit at breakneck speed. In no time we came upon the animal
whose tracks we had not been able to recognize. It was, of all
things, a leopard seal, fifty miles from the nearest salt water at
Goodhope Bay. The seal showed fight and the dogs circled it
warily until Allockeok hit it with a shovel, killing it instantly.
The animal, which must have weighed more than a hundred
pounds normally, was as light as a rabbit. It was down to skin
and bones and all the hair on its underparts had been worn off.
As near as we could guess it had been basking on the ice and
its blowhole had iced over or had been lost somehow so that the
seal could not get back in the water. Then, instead of going out
to sea, it had headed southwest and was going overland in search
of open water. Allockeok said it was following the sun and that
this was not the first time seals had been found inland, but it
was the only instance of the kind that I had ever heard of.

We found the sheet metal building that we were to dismantle
and while occupied at this chore, spent several days with Nick
Nicon, a Greek who was mining nearby on Dick Creek. He proudly
showed us nuggets and coarse gold he had taken from his property, some so large he referred to them as *oranges*. He was not
mining yet; just digging out his equipment from the snowdrifts
to be in readiness for the coming thaw. The only water Nick had
to sluice his gravel with was from the melting snow so this
limited his mining activity to only two or three weeks a season.
But in that time he took enough gold out to keep him the rest of
the year which he usually spent in Nome. He never got rich
though, and I understand he spent his last years in the Pioneer's
Home in Sitka.

By the time we got the building down, the snow was beginning to thaw so we had to hurry back to Shishmaref while there
was still enough for sledding. We got home on the seventh of May.

Chapter XXII

FINDING HOMES FOR OUR PETS

Toni and I had mailed in our resignations effective June 30, 1925, and planned to take off for Nome by some means or other as soon as navigation opened which usually was the first week in July at that place. So we began to think about homes for our pets which we would have to leave behind. Red, our malemute bitch, was no problem. She was a perfect specimen which we had reared from a pup. She had a reddish coat, tipped in black, somewhat like a red fox. The arches of her feet were high, her legs straight and strong and the fur on her flanks was thick. Allockeok had spoken for her with the idea of using her to build up the strain of his sled dogs which had suffered from cross breeding with *outside* dogs. Many of the Shishmaref malemutes had such thin fur on their flanks that they would freeze on the trail unless they were equipped with flank protectors. Others had spindly, crooked legs with splay feet resulting from mongrel crosses. We had become attached to Red as she was the most intelligent animal we had ever seen but we knew it would be best for her to stay and we were confident Allockeok would treat her right.

Our cat was a different story. It didn't take us long to find that we had made a dreadful mistake in taking a lone tabby cat to a remote island where there were no other cats, especially tom cats. Even a wild cat or a Canadian lynx might have solved her difficulties but sadly, there were no felines of any description in the area. In desperation she tried to make love to the malemutes but they would have nothing to do with her. She even flirted with Red who, not understanding her problem, dismissed her as a wanton Lesbian feline, picked her up by the scruff of her neck, carried her out the door and dropped her.

One day I spread the word around the village that I would give the cat to anyone who wanted her and if there were no takers I was going to take it out on the ice and shoot it. Early next morning there was a rap at our door. Standing there was a boy about twelve years old who looked me steadily in the eye and said, "I want cat." Now, to these Eskimos, a cat was a curious and undoubtedly valuable animal. They could hardly believe that I would actually give it away, much less shoot it. But Freddie

Azgayak was surprised and delighted when he found I meant it and proudly carried the cat to his igloo. Eskimos have cat food of all descriptions, especially fish and seal liver, so what the frustrated feline lacked in love life, she made up in high living. The last time we saw her she was basking in the sun on top the igloo out of reach of the malemutes and fat as a seal. For the time being, at least, she was perfectly happy.

Chapter XXIII

AN EXPERIENCE IN FREEZING

On the thirteenth day of May the first oogruk of the season was brought in so we knew spring was definitely on the way and soon our picturesque *winter Eskimos* would again be the drab, sun tanned, squint-eyed marine hunters they were when we first saw them two years earlier. One of the boys suggested we take a hunt on the mainland before the inlet ice went out or was flooded by fresh water from the hinterland which was just beginning to flow seaward.

The ice looked white in the direction of Cape Kruzenstern, which is a good sign, so we headed for the point hoping to get an early goose or at least some ptarmigan. Had the ice looked black it would have revealed the presence of water on the ice which we would have to avoid or get in trouble, even in May, as our daily temperatures were still well below zero on the coast.

For most of the way the ice was dry and we made good time. At one place it was so clear we actually saw a school of herring in it, frozen solid. The fish looked alive, all headed the same direction, evenly spaced and at different depths. I should have liked to chop out a block and brought it into the village to thaw out and to test the theory that fish so frozen can be revived. But we had no saw or axe and were in a hurry anyway so we passed up the opportunity to serve science for the dubious sport that lay ahead.

Just before we reached land we encountered fresh water overflowing the ice which indicated the Serpentine was thawing. It was only a few inches deep so we continued on, reluctant to turn back just a few hundred feet short of our goal. But the nearer we came to the cape, the deeper the water got. The last hundred yards saw us floating the sled, the dogs swimming, and us wading in water boots, knee deep. The water was obviously rising fast so we allowed ourselves only half an hour ashore. Hunting geese was out of the question with so little time so we satisfied ourselves by bagging a dozen or so ptarmigan then descended the bluff to where our dogs and sled had been left.

We had returned none too soon, in fact, not soon enough. The water was now waist deep so our hip-length mukluks were useless. The dogs swam the stretch easily and shook themselves dry as soon as they got out. We hooked them to the sled and took off for the village ten miles away. We had no change so our clothing froze immediately. In the two hours that followed I experienced a sensation of internal chill that I had never felt before or since. For the first time in my life, I became conscious of my skeleton. Mentally, I could feel each bone in my arms and legs. In the same way, I could count my ribs. My head became a skull and I could feel the roots of all my teeth. My face seemed especially bony. I had never dreamed there were so many bones there. My hip joints functioned all right but I could not bend my knees and this had me worried. The ice on which we were walking was as level as a floor and I could cross this stiff-legged if need be. But when we should reach the island we would have to cross a bit of tundra that would rise some fifteen feet to the top of the dunes on which the village rested. How would we do that? My hunting companion wasn't saying anything and neither was I. But we were both thinking.

At last we reached the island. By that time I had visions of gangrene, amputations and all those tragic results of freezing that I had heard about. This, I thought, was likely my last trip.

Getting up on the island was accomplished by picking a route along the course of a summer rivulet which was a uniform rise, and walking stiff-legged by swinging first one leg in an arc then the other until we reached the village. I then had Toni fill a tub with cold water and douse my lower extremities with water until I could bend my knees and get into the tub. It was not long until my clothing thawed out enough to get out of them and presently the frost began to leave me, too. It was painful at first but my freezing had produced no ill effects thanks to the cold water treatment. Of course, most of my freezing was in my water-soaked clothes but at the time I could not distinguish myself from my garments. The Eskimo boy suffered no ill effects either and neither did the dogs but it would have been different had we been obliged to spend the night out.

Chapter XXIV

SPRINGTIME IN THE ARCTIC

June is the fine time in the Arctic and since we had few regular duties to perform now that school was closed and the people were dispersed, we lived an idyllic life. There were twenty-four hours of daylight with clear skies and temperatures up to sixty degrees Fahrenheit. The winds had ceased, flowers bloomed everywhere and there were no mosquitos or insects of any kind. Birds were nesting on all sides, not only small song birds like the longspurs, but ducks, geese, gulls, terns, loons, jaegers, swans and ptarmigan. On the fourteenth we paddled a small skinboat over to a flat island in the lagoon about a mile from the village and gathered gull eggs for our second wedding anniversary dinner the following day. Most of them were incubating but we had enough fresh ones for our purposes. Tern eggs were by far the best, being small and delicate in flavor, but we were reluctant to gather them since it took so many to equal one hen's egg. We never disturbed the ptarmigan nests and took very few goose eggs, but gull eggs we considered legitimate since there were so many and the gulls were in no danger of extinction.

We painted the schoolhouse and the teacher's cottage in the hopes of leaving the station for the next occupants a little better than we had found it. Then we took inventory, repaired equipment and furniture and brought the station reports such as vital statistics up to date. Every few days we would take off, either north or south, to visit the oogruk camps that had been set up every mile or so along the ocean beach. The shore ice was gone but the pack was still there a short distance off shore and extending twenty miles or so out to sea. It was already fractured in many places and in these cracks and leads the hunters were killing oogruk and seals. Several men had set out gill nets and were getting a few salmon that were probably heading for Kotzebue Sound as they didn't enter our local creeks and rivers.

Once as we were approaching a cluster of tents and drying racks that constituted an oogruk camp we heard a cry then saw a man rush out of a tent and dash over a sand dune that stood between the camp and the sea. We reached the top of the dune in time to see the man pick up a kayak and launch it like a boy would a sled. In less than a split minute he had reached his partner who was struggling in the icy water. The man about to be rescued was the victim of an accident, having capsized his kayak as he was throwing a bag of sand overboard to anchor his gill net. Few Eskimos have ever learned to swim but even a good swimmer would have been paralyzed in these chill waters in a very few minutes. The Eskimo *buddy system* has probably saved many lives for in the Arctic a lone man is in constant danger of losing his life, a life that may often be saved if a companion be present.

On these walks we often picked up pieces of old ivory for our collection or bartered with the natives for things which they had lately found in the region of their camps. In two years our accumulation of curios had filled a trunk even though we had decided to take not more than one of each type of artifact. Our treasures now included a coal black walrus tusk and an equally black mammoth tusk. We had another small mammoth tusk of several shades of brown and a pair of white walrus tusks, on one of which I had engraved a pictorial story of our trip to Shishmaref. Then we had a jade spoon, a jade burnisher or whetstone, a jade harpoon head and an ivory drill bow of great age, engraved with hunting scenes, etc. The collection included flint arrowheads, trade beads from the Orient, wearing apparel, tools, and several bags of eider down. Another treasure was a small ivory man doll. Its face was ornamented with two tiny copper labrets and it was yellowed with age. I was told it had been a shaman's doll and the fact that it was worn quite thin in the middle from handling or rubbing seemed to verify this information.

*   *   *   *

Each winter lofty pressure ridges form in the ice along the coast a short distance offshore. This ice becomes grounded in the shallow water and remains there for a time after the ice pack breaks up and drifts away. Storms and ordinary ground swells cause this ice to plow up the bottom. Then bits of ivory, sea shells, crystals and bone are cast on the beach during each subsequent blow. As soon as we became apprized of this sequence we made regular beachcombing excursions along the shore of our island and often returned with several pounds of assorted materials. These included fragments of ivory, shells of snails, whelks and clams of species unfamiliar to us, pyrite nodules, calcite pseudomorphs, and well-preserved teeth of pleistocene horses, oxen and other ungulata. At the time, of course, we hadn't

the slightest idea what they were beyond the fact that they were
teeth but we kept them until we could check them out. It was
on rambles like this that we found out how little we actually
knew for sure, and how necessary it was for us to return to
school to try to find out some of the answers.

On June 20 I was invited to accompany a party of natives
who were going up the Serpentine for a little holiday before the
mosquitos came. They seemed mostly concerned with resting
and absorbing sunshine which had considerably more warmth
away from the sea than it did on our narrow islet. But they gill-
netted some grayling and ling and gathered eggs for daily use.
I roamed the tundra, alone, looking for exotic plants and exam-
ining countless nests of owls, loons, ducks, geese and ptarmigan.
What a wonderful place a tundra is in springtime before the
mosquitos hatch. And what a hell on earth they can make it for
at least thirty days each summer. We had none of the insect
repellants so common today; in fact, we didn't even have
mosquito nets due to an oversight. So we will never forget or
forgive the insect billions that drove the reindeer into the sea
and almost drove us to suicide.

Two days after we left Shishmaref, the wind suddenly
shifted to the south so we knew the ice would soon go out. We
returned to the village on the twenty-fourth to find the sea open
and the cutter *Bear* in port, that is, standing in the roadstead a
mile or so offshore. Captain C. S. Cochran, who was command-
ing the *Bear* at that time, invited Toni and me aboard to tea. We
accepted the invitation almost reluctantly for in our mukluks
and semi-native habit we felt vastly inferior to the spit and polish
of the officers of the *Bear*, especially in the carpeted quarters of
the captain, luxuries strangely out of place in the Arctic.

During the course of our visit, Captain Cochran asked us to
tell him the meaning of the tall masts that stood at each end of
our island. We had put them up the year before, I told him, as
aids to the sea hunters who often had difficulty in locating the
village. One had alternate bands of black and white while the
other had a black and white spiral running its entire length. We
had made the masts, which were about fifty feet long, by splicing
several driftwood poles together. Each was topped by a triangle,
one pointing up, the other down. After I had finished, Captain
Cochran told us the markers had helped him find the village and
that so far as he knew they were the first aids to navigation in
the Alaskan Arctic.

The reason the *Bear* had called in was not exactly social. The news had gotten around that some of our boys had been getting out of hand lately regarding their attitudes to other men's wives and Captain Cochran had come to investigate the rumor and to remind the offenders about the law. In fact, we had received a complaint of this nature from a herder who alleged his wife, Annie, had been criminally attacked by one of these unattached fellows who periodically made the rounds of the isolated herd or trapper cabins, in hopes of finding a woman alone. We had reported the complaint to the U. S. Commissioner at Teller and a deputy U. S. Marshal had been sent up to Shishmaref to arrest the fellow and bring him to trial. The trial was held in Teller some days later. The accused man pleaded not guilty, asserting that he had merely been stormbound at the cabin. At night he had retired to his own sleeping bag. Later the woman had called to him and when he asked her what she wanted she said she only wanted to see if he was asleep. Whether or not an attack followed is academic. Where we lost the case was when Annie testified that in the ensuing encounter she had personally removed her pants because she was afraid he might tear them.

*   *   *   *

Aboard the *Bear* we found a party of Eskimos who were being returned to their homes at Point Hope. They were part of a group that had been placed a year or so earlier on Wrangel Island in an attempt at colonization of this controversial island. The Russians had taken them off and now they were being repatriated in Alaska after a roundabout trip through Siberia, Japan, and a winter in Seattle. I photographed the first child ever born there, in the arms of its mother, on the decks of the *Bear*.

The ship left that night but was back again the twenty-sixth, having gotten within fifty miles of Kotzebue whose roadstead was still blocked with ice. It continued on to the south, presumably to Teller. The next day the wind shifted to the north and Shishmaref was again icebound. On the twenty-ninth we saw the *Bear* heading north again but on the thirtieth we made out her smoke on the horizon, southbound. She had given up her third attempt to reach Kotzebue that season.

Chapter XXV

THIRTY-THREE DAYS TO SEATTLE

We had been planning to leave our station as soon after June 30 as possible since our resignations were effective that day. We expected to go to Nome on the mailboat *Nokatak* and catch the *Victoria* there for Seattle. But, since we had no post office, her call at Shishmaref was by courtesy only and then only when the weather was fair. She did call northbound on the second of July and we made arrangements to board her southbound, weather permitting. She would be back in a week so we started packing. Most of our chattels, guns, phonograph and records, etc., we either sold or gave away, keeping only our curios and *outside* clothing. All of our skin and fur wardrobe was left behind. Two large trunks were packed to follow us on any craft they could be put aboard. A small steamer trunk and two suitcases were packed to accompany us if we were lucky enough to get passage.

The Fourth of July came and we celebrated in solitude by walking to the end of our island. Funny how meaningless an important holiday can be unless there are people around with the will to make something of it. Without heat, dust, bands, bunting, baseball and barbecues, firecrackers, pink lemonade, hot dogs and hamburgers, Independence Day was a dud so far as we were concerned. And if there had been any Eskimos in town I doubt that we could have conjured up any enthusiasm about our having freed ourselves from the British some 149 years previously, anyway.

A few days later a storm came up and we saw a rocking, rolling *Nokatak* slipping by without a chance in the world of making a landing. And with her went our hopes of getting out in time to catch the *Victoria*.

Luck of a sort was with us, however, for our fox-farming friend, Percy Blatchford, having broken with his associate, was moving his equipment to Teller. He wanted to send a native boy, Orville, to Teller by dory with a load consisting of five malemute puppies but was reluctant to send him off, alone. He suggested that we go together since there might not be another chance to get out all summer. The idea sounded good to us as we were now champing at the bit. The weather was still stormy but we kidded

Eddie Tocktoo and family.

A well-dressed woman.

All dressed up for a picture.

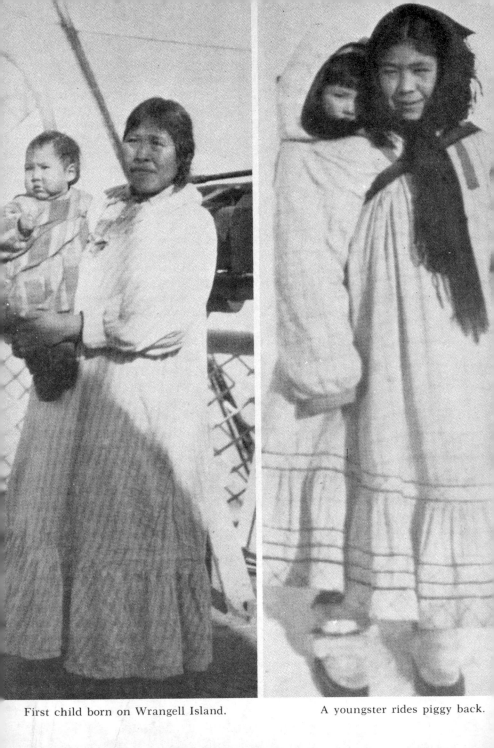

First child born on Wrangell Island.   A youngster rides piggy back.

An Eskimo Madonna.

The Nayokpuk family. He was our storekeeper and my trail companion.

Proud mama and kids.

The Ahgupuk family—All present except George, the artist.

Posed for a picture.

Small fry in winter garb.

Wm. Armstrong—the man who saved the mail . . . and two Shishmaref belles.

Five Shishmaref belles.

This house was above ground.

Shishmaref in winter dress.

An oomiak on its winter rack.

Main Street . . . Shishmaref in early fall.

Toni and "Red" on a typical sod igloo.

A tomcod fisherwoman.

Fishing through the ice.

UNITED STATES MARSHAL'S OFFICE.

SECOND DIVISION, DISTRICT OF ALASKA

Nome, Alaska, Sept 18th, 1925.

Bureau of Education,

      Seattle, Washington.

Gentlemen;-

      Enclosed find check NO 0003987 of Sept 16th, 1925, amount $ 16.50 favor Edward L Keithahn for services as Special Deputy in case of the United States vs John Radoontsoff and Ed Cross.

      Kindly deliver or forward same to him; your Supt- Range at this point advises us this is the best procedure to obtain delivery of this check.

      Respectfully,

      Chas D Jones,

      United States Marshal

R/

How I drew my salary as special deputy.

Toni and the team.

Toni

This was a gag shot although I regularly used all the outfit except the fez.

Little Eskimo brothers.

ourselves into believing it was getting better. At nine-thirty that evening, with a small party of friends standing by and assuring us we were foolish, we shoved off and headed down the coast.

Our *ship* was a twelve or fourteen-foot Wagner-built dory with a well near the stern to accommodate a two and one-half horsepower outboard motor. For mast and boom we had two long oomiak oars or *sweeps*. Our sail was square, Eskimo-style, but we made good time with it in a favorable wind. Our freight, besides the pups, consisted of our sleeping bags, the steamer trunk wrapped in canvas, and fairly waterproof, and suitcases, gasoline, and grub box with a week's provisions.

The Chukchi sea is shallow and because of this changes can come rapidly. We had hardly gotten underway when a stiff wind sprang up and almost immediately Toni and all the pups were actively seasick. So Orville and I decided to take the boat into the lagoon where it was quiet, by way of the channel at the lower end of our island. It was our luck to attempt this just as the tide was running its strongest. Pouring out of the lagoon like a mill race against the wind, it set up rips that stood up and lapped above our little craft menacingly. At last we reached the sheltered waters and our passengers soon recovered. I was really scared as I had never navigated tide rips before, but seeing that the Eskimo boy paid no attention, looking neither left nor right, I took courage and steered through to safety. Later I asked Orville if he had been afraid. He said no, he wasn't, but he would have been except that he noticed that I wasn't worried and that had given him courage.

The lagoon was already too shallow for our outboard motor but we could use our sail. However, as the tide continued to run out we soon found our boat dragging bottom, so we had to get out and push for a spell. Eventually the tide changed, the water came back, and the sea having quieted down somewhat, we sneaked out through a channel and tried the open ocean again. We were now about twenty-five miles southeast of Shishmaref. It was eight a.m. so it had taken about eleven hours to come this far, hardly as fast as a walk. But now a northwest wind sprang up and the sea got choppier, then big swells began to roll under us and we could see the shoreline getting whiter by the minute. Something told us that if we wanted to land right side up, we had better head for the beach now. We made our landing through the surf some forty miles from Shishmaref in the vicinity of

Ikpik. Our sail provided a tent and we had a pleasant sleep on the tundra just off the beach.

Early the next morning we shoved off again. A low surf was breaking on the beach but we got through and into deep water without too much difficulty. However, we had gone only a few miles when the wind picked up and we found it prudent to head for shore again. This time a bluff prevented us from dragging our dory off the beach so we turned it on edge for a shelter, using the sail for a floor. Exploring our campsite we found the high ground above the bluff covered with the ruins of many igloos. It was the long-deserted village of *Esook* that I had passed many times in the winter but had never seen uncovered. All about were fragments of bentwood boxes, wooden dishes and spoons, all bleached a uniform silver gray. I searched in vain for something from white man's culture and concluded the site must be very old, having been abandoned before our time. For a souvenir of the site I picked up a wooden mask in the form of a rabbit's head. The Eskimo boy showed immediate disapproval of my removing the mask, hinting darkly that it would bring bad luck. I laughed off his fears and carried my long-eared trophy into camp.

Next morning things began to happen. First, when we were trying to get our dory through the surf, an oversized comber caught us sideways and flipped us over. Fortunately all of our duffle came ashore and we were able to salvage it, that is, all except our grub. As a matter of fact, all we had left was a small bag of dried apples that I was carrying in my cloth parka pocket to munch on. Sea water swelled them up, bursting the bag, but we found them edible when we got hungry enough. We skidded the dory up the beach as far as we could then took off our clothes, wrung them out, and put them on again. There was no way to dry out our reindeer skin sleeping bags, so we crawled in any-way, since there was no other way to get warm while it rained and blew.

The next four or five days blended into one as there was no nightfall or other changes that could separate the hours into days. At first we felt a hollowness about the midsection and a few pangs of hunger when the dried apples were gone. We had a rifle and a few shells but the storm had driven all the ducks and ptarmigan inland. Our last shells were spent trying to shoot passing gulls on the wing. The pups foraged up and down the beach, cracking whelks like bones, but getting thinner by the day. We were probably losing weight, too, but the only thing we noticed was that we were getting weaker. We no longer felt hungry but had an overpowering desire to sleep. Consequently we spent most of the time in the bags whose hides had swelled and whose hair was now beginning to slip.

What had been going on in Orville's mind, I don't know, as he seldom spoke. Each day Toni and I would beachcomb the north shore and he would go south but neither of us found anything to eat. One evening Orville split up my mask and burned it without a word. There was such a look of determination on his face I decided not to comment.

Next day the storm continued, combers seven to eight feet tall breaking on the beach with monotonous rhythm. Toni and I took off as usual to make our daily inspection of the beach. We had not gone far when we saw something ahead lying in the sand. Upon approaching it closer we saw that it was a young hair seal that apparently had been cast ashore by the surf and hadn't been able to get back in. But just then the seal saw us and made a mad lunge for the comber that was just beginning to break over it. I dashed up with my club and got in a lucky blow just as the seal was disappearing in the froth. For the first time in my life, I knew the joy of the primitive hunter who kills to live and not for sport. Happily we carried the seal back to camp and simultaneously we felt a return of the will to survive. It is a curious thing that up until now, the question of survival hadn't entered our minds but neither had despair. We had just been too drowsy to care, one way or another.

Orville came in empty-handed as usual shortly after we got in, looking gaunt and dejected but we saw his eyes brighten when he saw the seal. He didn't mention it by way of rubbing it in, but I'm sure he knew that he had changed our luck by burning the mask. That day we dined on seal liver and flippers and never did sandy, unsalted seal taste better. What we didn't eat we cooked for the pups and when we all got through there was nothing left, not even for a seagull.

Our luck had indeed changed. Next day Orville found three dead seals and a decapitated walrus. But best of all, the wind suddenly changed and began blowing offshore. Hurriedly, to take advance of this change of affairs, we loaded up and pushed the dory into the water, this time with no surf to buck. We set our sail and got the little outboard motor started. The wind was fresh and we fairly raced down the coast, the spray drenching us and slopping into the boat. Then a blast of hurricane strength carried away our sail and nearly capsized the dory. We cut the sail loose and bailed furiously with oil cans cut in half but couldn't keep up. The boat was taking water unaccountably so we were forced to run for shore. Then a wave broke over the dory and one cylinder of our motor quit. The other kept going though, so with the help of the oars, we finally got the waterlogged craft into shallow water whereupon Orville and I jumped out and towed it in.

When we rolled the dory over to make our customary shelter we saw why our boat had persisted in sinking. Somehow, all the caulking had worked out and cracks a quarter of an inch wide had opened up its full length. We re-caulked the seams with whatever we could find then lay down to figure out our next move.

During the night wind had changed again and without letting up began to blow a gale from the northwest. Simultaneously the surf took up its roar and we were right back where we had been a week earlier. Then an over-sized comber broke on the beach and its water ran into our shelter and lifted us in our sleeping bags. That was too much. When we got wrung out again Orville and I were all for making a try to get through the surf but Toni objected and we couldn't get her into the dory. Just to show her how easily it could be done now that we had experience, we left her on the beach and took the dory off for a demonstration run. We got through the first three or four lines of breakers then suddenly the granddaddy of them all stood up before us like a black moving wall. Our boat was upended and Orville and I leaped out to left and right. The dory came in end over end and so did we. As soon as our feet struck the beach we ran out from under the nearest comber and grabbed the boat so the undertow wouldn't carry it out again. Thus ended the demonstration. But we were so sure of ourselves we tried it three more times with Toni in there with us before we gave up the idea that we could master a boiling sea. Licked, we retreated to the dunes, wrung out our clothes, put them on again and crawled into our sodden sacks.

Then we got a better idea. We had noticed that the runback from these jumbo-sized breakers provided enough water to float the dory. So we recaulked the boat, loaded up, and started dragging it down the shore just inside the breakers. Toni and the pups walked and eventually we all arrived at a channel leading into Lopp Lagoon. We finally got into the still waters of the lagoon then followed the shore until we came to a reindeer camp of the

Wales herders. There were a few women and children about and from them we got a supply of reindeer meat. Then we took over a deserted igloo nearby and spent the next day drying our clothes and feasting on venison, a welcome diversion from seal.

We were most reluctant to leave this place for in contrast to what we had lately been through here was a place where one could spend the rest of his life. It had quit raining, the sun was bright and warm. We were sheltered from wind and far from the noisy surf. Songbirds filled the air and the tundra was dotted with sweet-scented, beautiful flowers of many colors. The food was good and there were no mosquitos to speak of. What more could one ask?

But dreams of an idyllic life on Lopp Lagoon soon gave place to stern reality. We were going home, to the States, and moreover we had a load of puppies to deliver to Teller. The next day found us heading out into the sea and the funnel that is Bering Strait.

I used to think that Bering Strait was all of that water intervening between Siberia and Alaska that was covered by those two words as printed on the maps. But going through in a dory you get a different impression. It is a relatively short channel in which you can feel the pull of the current like that of a strong magnet. We felt it the minute it hit us, repelling us and forcing us back. It was hard to buck with our little motor but we got through and almost to the village when our outboard motor gave up the ghost. We took to the oars and started to row ashore but the strong current carried us back three miles before we made the beach. There was nothing to do but drag our boat to a safe place and walk the three miles back to Wales where we anticipated some of the luxuries of civilization.

*   *   *   *

Wales turned out to be somewhat of a disappointment. There were no people there. The town was one hundred per cent deserted. People, of course, didn't matter so much. What we wanted was food and shelter so we headed for the schoolhouse. It was locked up but we gained access through an unguarded window, feeling almost apologetic for entering what with our salt and sand-incrusted clothing, whiskers, and general crumminess. But there was no one to apologize to, so we moved in.

We didn't find any food in the house excepting a bag of wheat that must have been left over when the chickens that belonged to the late Wales teachers froze. Down in the marsh behind the schoolhouse we found a patch of sourdock which we gathered, and that was it. Our first civilized meal in Wales consisted of boiled chicken feed and boiled sourdock. But it was a welcome diversion from the all-meat menu we had had since the dried apples gave out. And we ate it off a table, seated on chairs, with a hard floor underfoot.

Upstairs we found something that got us wondering. It was a huge cowhide trunk and across its top was lettered *Roald Amundsen*. I don't know what we were thinking but subconsciously something was saying that here is Amundsen's trunk and sooner or later he will come for it and when he does there might be a chance for us to get to Nome. Anyway, Tin City was just over the mountain from Wales, so next day we went over the mountain to find out what they knew there.

Wales Mountain is not so high, perhaps 2000 feet, but from its upper slopes you get a wonderful view of the Diomede Islands which lie midway in Bering Strait and the Siberian coast beyond, just fifty-six miles from Wales. It is a rocky mountain suggesting some giant had taken house-sized boulders and heaped them up. In the scanty patches of soil we found clusters of arctic poppies in bloom but that was about the only vegetation, save moss and lichens. Our mukluks were ideal for this sort of mountain climbing as the soles were so thin and flexible that we could almost grab and hold on with our feet, monkey-wise, and the straw lining protected us from stone bruises. But they provided no ankle support and I suppose they would have worn out much faster than cowhide or rubber.

In Tin City we found the tin mine operating full blast with a native crew from Wales. The Christensen family who operated the mine took us in and there we found the answer to the Amundsen trunk mystery. It seems that a couple of years or so previously Amundsen had taken the two Carpenter girls from East Cape, Siberia, to Norway for their education. When it came time for them to return home, Amundsen had sent them from Norway to Seattle where they boarded Captain John Backlund's sailing ship, the *C. S. Holmes*, which annually went to the Arctic on a trading trip. Backlund had taken the girls as far as Wales and had put them ashore there with their luggage. So it was their effects and not Amundsen's in the Amundsen cowhide trunk. The Christensens had gone over the mountain to Wales a few days earlier for their mail, and finding the girls there alone had taken them home with them until a way could be found to get them over to the Siberian side. We met the girls who were half East Cape Eskimo and half white, but since they had been educated in Norway and spoke no English, we could not converse with them like the Christensens could. How they eventually got home we never learned. It was no easy matter for, even then, few American skippers would risk a trip into Russian waters.

The Christensens, who were the pioneer tin miners of Alaska, were most hospitable and we enjoyed our brief visit with them. We also had a chance to do a little panning in the tin placers there and to learn for the first time what *cassiterite* looks like. But while we were there the Eskimo crew suddenly got tired of their job or the food or something else and quit without notice. The next day they went over the hump to Wales and we trailed along with them.

When we broke over the summit and looked down on Wales we saw a mysterious-looking little schooner lying at anchor in the roadstead. The hull had been painted black once but now it was gray and streaked, looking like something the high tide had lifted out of a boneyard. The surf was still too strong for a landing and none of the Eskimos were very anxious to go out to her.

The following day I managed to talk a group of natives into attempting to reach the schooner by lining a skinboat up to the point from which we could drift down to the ship with little risk or trouble. We found the schooner to be the *Twins*, a thirty-footer or so, out of Siberia bound for Nome. The skipper, Ed Gross, an American citizen of Nome, had gone to Siberia some years prior, to prospect in the Kolyma River country several hundred miles west of East Cape. Apparently he had done all right for a time as the country was rich in gold and fur. But then the effects of the Revolution began to be felt in the far corners of the former Russian Empire. A band of *Reds* would suddenly appear, exterminate what *Whites* they could find and collect taxes. Then a band of *Whites* would appear and liquidate the *Reds* whereupon they, too, would collect taxes. Then the *Reds* would come back and repeat the process. Gross was allowed to mine but his profits, if any, all belonged to the Government, be it *Red* or *White*. Gross tried to leave the country and somehow or other got as far as Anadyr, south of the Cape, but was detained there in a sort of house arrest.

Here Gross laid his plans for escape to Alaska and, plotting with him, were two Russian citizens. One, by the name of John Radoonstoff, had been an officer in the Imperial army during the Revolution. The other, a Caucasian Mohammedan by the name of Movrza Bek Dzedzveff, was believed to be a counterfeiter by the others and was a fugitive out of Vladivostok seeking asylum in America.

Gross couldn't get permission to sail for Alaska but he finally wangled clearance for East Cape. But just to be sure that he went there and not some other place, the authorities at Anadyr had put two armed guards aboard. How Gross got rid of the guards I doubt that I will ever know for sure. He told us he caught them off guard, disarmed them and put them ashore. At least he had their firearms, a Russian army rifle and an army revolver unusual to me in that the bullets were entirely inside the cases instead of protruding from them.

Once free of the guards, Gross had set a course for St. Lawrence Island, the nearest American land to the Gulf of Anadyr. But when he arrived at the island village of Savoonga, the Government schoolteacher stationed there informed him that he could not land the Russians there. In other words, to come home himself, Gross must first return his shipmates to Russian territory. Learning this, the Caucasian jumped ship and tried to hide out on the island. But he was soon captured and returned to the ship which thereupon set sail for Big Diomede Island where the captain hoped to land him. At this point the Caucasian seized the army rifle and a cache of food and barricaded himself in the bilge. Gross and Radoonstoff had the pistol, however, on deck so it was even-steven. He couldn't get out of the bilge to take over the ship and they couldn't go near the hatch for fear of being shot. Neither did any of the three dare go to sleep. That was the story we heard when we boarded the *Twins*, and at that point none had had a wink of sleep for ten days.

Gross was surprised to learn where he was from me as he had been completely lost in fog and storm and didn't even have a compass. Hoping to get a lift to Nome I asked Gross what his intentions were. He said he would go over to Big Diomede, the Russian island, as soon as the storm let up and smoke the mutineer out with the fire extinguisher and put him ashore. We never questioned his ability to do that and made arrangements for him to pick us up on his return to the Alaskan side. Apparently he had decided to risk bringing Radoonstoff in, regardless of the consequences, since without an ally, he had slim hopes of dealing with the Mohammedan. Dzedzveff had boasted of his criminal past and had threatened Gross's life so there was no point in trying to get him into the United States. Big Diomede, which at that time had no Russian inhabitants, was about the only place Gross could dump him and not be captured himself.

All next day it stormed and the *Twins* continued to ride at anchor. But the following day we saw its flag flying upside down, at half mast. What had happened aboard we didn't know, but we got a crew together as fast as we could and started out. It was then that we noticed that the *Twins* was drifting and headed for the rocks. We got aboard barely in time to prevent a wreck. Gross was pretty upset when we came on deck. He told us the mutineer had deliberately tried to wreck the ship by picking a hole through the hull and sawing off the anchor line with a keyhole saw. When Gross had tried to put out the spare anchor he had come up with the rifle and threatened him. Upon our approach he had crawled back to his hideout and we were able to put out the anchor just in time.

But now Gross was really worried. He suddenly realized that his idea of smoking out the mutineer was just so much *happy talk*. In actual practice, it couldn't be done, not with that single soda and acid extinguisher, anyway. And then, out of the blue, he asked *me* to get him out.

I was not then and am still definitely not the hero type. I look upon heroics as something generally compounded out of stupidity and exhibitionism plus a certain lack of the instinct of self-preservation. But I undertook the job simply because I thought it was safe for me even though it was probably sure death for Gross or Radoonstoff. I asked Radoonstoff to tell Dzedzveff that there was a missionary aboard and to see if he wanted to talk to him. Radoonstoff shouted something in Russian that I couldn't understand. Then from the bowels of the ship I heard an anxious voice shout something back, the only word of which I recognized was the broken equivalent of *missionary*. Radoonstoff was bobbing his head up and down, his eyes beaming, saying, "Yes, he wants to see you. It's all right for you to go down!"

I took hold of the hatch combing and dropped to the bottom where bilgewater was sloshing around large boulders carried for ballast. It was dark down there but gradually things began to take form. First I saw a pair of large Russian leather boots stretched out on the rocks in front of me. Then I saw that they were occupied by a rather small, black-bearded man lying on his back, his head and shoulders resting on a bundle of deer skins. Beside him lay the rifle pointing in my direction. The man seemed done in and didn't interfere when I drew the rifle to me and tossed it on a pile of furs out of reach of either of us. I then took hold of his ankles and drew him out into the light of the hatchway. With a little help and persuasion, I got him to stand up, whereupon Gross and Radoonstoff, reaching down from above, lifted him up to the deck. They immediately began to pummel him unmercifully and I had to land a few on them before I could get them to quit. When they had cooled down a little I told them to rope him hand and foot, and supervised the job myself when I found them doing a slipshod job. In addition to binding the wrists and ankles, I had them bind his elbows securely whereupon we placed him in a bunk across from the captain's berth.

Gross now felt happy and immensely relieved. He rewarded all of us for our help, giving each Eskimo a fine tanned Siberian deerskin. For Toni, he presented me with two dozen fine ermine skins, each bearing a Russian stamp that attested the tax had been paid at least once. He told us he would sleep until midnight then run over to Big Diomede and dump his prisoner. He would then return to Wales and pick us up before going on to Nome.

The storm having died out, it looked as if Gross would get away as planned so Orville and I went down to the channel to get our dory and bring it in to Wales to be ready to leave upon Gross's return. It must have been close to midnight when we rounded the point as the low red sun was due north. But suddenly a brilliant light flared up on the forward deck of the *Twins*, which was still a mile or so away. As we watched it wondering what was up, the fiery mass suddenly hurtled into the sea and a huge column of black smoke arose. In a few moments the same procedure was repeated. We were now certain someone on the ship was trying to signal the village for help but from our distance we could see no one on deck.

Since we were approaching from the west we doubted that we had been seen by anyone watching the village which lay north of the anchored ship. So we inscribed an arc in our course to approach the ship from the south, just in case. Nobody was on deck as we came alongside, but as I grasped the guardrail I saw the deck was spattered with blood. Just then Gross came around the corner of the pilot house. A towel was wrapped around his head, turban-like, and several broad streaks of blood coursed his otherwise chalky face. Before he could say anything, Radoon-stoff's head popped out of the hatch, and he vaulted onto the deck, rifle in hand. He seemed entirely insane for the moment, yelling gibberish, and moving his rifle from left to right like a machine gun, apparently mowing down imaginary enemies.

It took some time to quiet them down enough to get a straight story. But what had happened was something like this. First, the prisoner had complained that his wrist ropes were cutting him and Gross had foolishly loosened them. Then he had stationed Radoonstoff on deck armed with the pistol, to guard. Gross thereupon crawled into his bunk across the aisle from his prisoner to get a little sleep before casting off for Big Diomede.

Sometime later, when Gross was asleep and Radoonstoff apparently dozing, the prisoner got his hands free. Taking a hatchet out of a tool box beneath Gross's bunk he made two murderous passes at the Captain's bald head. But because his elbows were still tied he could not make a fatal stroke. He cleaved the skull but not through it. At that point Radoonstoff must have awakened and from his post immediately above the two berths, saw what was happening. He fired a couple shots, and the prisoner flung the hatchet at him, at the same time dashing back to his former hideaway in the bilge. Gross was so confused, having been attacked in his sleep, he thought Radoonstoff had shot him and had to be told that he had been axed and that the prisoner was loose.

After Radoonstoff had got the captain's wounds bound up they began trying to attract attention in the village. First they had fired the rifle several times but everyone had gone to bed and igloos are practically sound-proof, anyway. Then they had filled a bucket with oily waste and set it afire on the bow. When that got too hot they had heaved it overboard and then lit another. That explained what we had seen from the dory. While they were still trying to get help from the village, they heard the escaped prisoner picking at the lock on the captain's trunk. Gross knew the trunk contained a loaded automatic pistol. There was only one thing left to do: get the prisoner before he got the automatic. Radoonstoff, rising to the situation, seized the rifle, leaped into the hatch and shot the mutineer dead just as we were coming aboard.

In order to be sure that we were getting a straight story I took a candle and went below. The body was crumpled over the captain's trunk beside which lay the pick. The damaged lock had held. Beside the body was the rope that had bound his elbows. Later, I found the wrist rope in the bunk. Radoonstoff yanked off the victim's shirt like he was skinning a rabbit. Then I saw that one of the pistol bullets had hit its mark, breaking the left shoulder. The rifle bullet, which must have been soft-nosed, had practically torn the right arm off at the shoulder. I felt ill and also somewhat remorseful for the little Caucasian who, in a few short days in his mad scramble to escape Siberia, had jumped ship, mutinied, attempted shipwreck and murder, and now lay mangled and dead only a few hundred yards from the promised land.

We carried the body up on deck, placed it in the skiff, and covered it with a piece of canvas. Then we took the captain ashore to see what we could do about his wounds. I also promised Radoonstoff I'd send out a couple of Eskimos, not so much as guards, but to keep Radoonstoff company during the night as he had no relish to spend it alone with the body of his late victim.

We found nothing at the schoolhouse to dress Gross's wounds but a bottle of iodine, which Toni poured on in the hopes it would keep the scalp healthy until we could find a doctor or a nurse who could sew up the three-inch slashes. Then we put Gross to bed upstairs and barricaded his door. We took this precaution since he was pacing the floor and raving like a madman. It might have been due to the pain, but the hatchet had penetrated the skull deeply and so far as we knew might have touched the brain. I had seen reindeer go berserk with brain injuries during corralling, so we were just taking no unnecessary chances.

Sometime during the early hours of the new day, Gross quieted down and we all got some sleep. Next morning he looked a little wan but rested, and the wound showed no signs of infection. We went out to the *Twins* after breakfast and hoisted our dory on deck. In a few minutes we had said goodbye to our Eskimo friends who had spent the night aboard ship and were on our way to Teller.

I wish I could say we had an uneventful trip for it is only sixty-odd miles from the Cape to Teller and in July it should have been an easy passage. But the *Twins* was underpowered and even with sails we lost headway every time the tide changed. And of course Toni was seasick again, so sick in fact that she didn't even complain when we made her a bed on deck beside the *sloopkie* carrying the corpse. Orville and I sailed the ship while Gross and Radoonstoff tried to make up ten nights' lost sleep. One would steer, and coax the motor while the other worked the sails and pumped. The only food aboard was a loaf of home-made bread of Gross's manufacture, I'm sure, and some over-ripe Siberian goose eggs. We made toast of the bread and fried the eggs on the top of the stove in just enough cylinder oil to keep them from sticking, there being no other grease of any kind aboard.

Twenty-two hours later we pulled in to Teller. It is small wonder that the populace of that little community stood aloof in little groups, silently watching us come in, and contemplating our flag which was hanging at half mast, upside down. Not until we spoke their names did our friends recognize us in our whiskers and grimy get-up.

Besides landing Orville and his pups, we now had other business at Teller. We went up to the home of Mrs. Billy Marx, who was the U. S. Commissioner, and told her our story. After all, she was the law west of Nome and we had business for her. However, Mrs. Marx sensed something international in our case and didn't want to handle it. Better, she said, that she deputize me a special U. S. Marshal, let me formally arrest the men and take them on to Nome for trial.

I had signed the papers deputizing me, before the trip to Nome was mentioned so there was no backing out. But I knew the old *Twins* was stuck together with nothing but reindeer tallow and sand, and leaking like a sieve. I dreaded taking her on to Nome in her semi-sinking condition. My friend, Tom Peterson, then came to my rescue with a fine idea.

"Why don't you tell her you have to pull the engine and overhaul it before you can make it to Nome?" he said. I thanked him for his co-operation and when Mrs. Marx agreed that I ought to have the motor repaired, we actually did pull it and take it into Tom's shop to work on it.

Then came the two breaks we had been stalling for. First, we got the glad news that the *Victoria* was coming right in to Teller for a load of reindeer meat and we could board it there and, second, the new mailboat, the *Silver Wave II*, was right ahead of her and aboard was a regular Deputy U. S. Marshal. We had long since given up catching the *Victoria*, but we learned that the day we thought it was due in Nome was the day it had sailed from Seattle. So in spite of all our delay we could still go home on the *Vic*. All that we had left to do in Alaska was to clear up the *Twins* affair that we had inadvertently become mixed up with.

Early next morning when the new *Silver Wave* came in I buttonholed the Marshal telling him what we had for him, my idea being to drop it all in his lap as soon as possible. He went aboard the *Twins* with me to have a look at the body which was now lying in about six inches of water. "It won't keep until we get to Nome," he said after one look. "We'll have to hold the inquest and bury the corpse here."

While the Marshal was having the body brought ashore, I went out and rounded up a jury. The inquest was held in a boat shed that afternoon and after Gross, Radoonstoff and I were questioned, the jury came up with a verdict of justifiable homicide and that was that. Dzedzveff was buried in the local potter's field and so far as Toni and I were concerned the case was closed. What happened to Gross and Radoonstoff is another story, one that didn't concern us, and whose outcome we never heard since the following day we left that part of the world forever.

Compared to the first three weeks of our journey home, the *Victoria* trip was uneventful. We stopped in Nome only two hours to pick up mail and passengers and at Akutan over night to take on a cargo of whale oil. On August thirteenth we entered Elliott Bay and saw the twinkling lights of Seattle that we had last seen just two years back. The journey home had taken thirty-three days, exactly what it had taken to get to our station. That first assignment was completed, but subsequent events were to reveal that it was only the beginning. In 1928 Toni and I returned to resume our work in Alaska. We're still at it after 40 years.

THE END